LeyL

 *a beginner's guide* 

PHILIP HESELTON

Hodder & Stoughton

A MEMBER OF THE HODDER HEADLINE GROUP

To those mentioned within who taught me so much about leys,
and to the English landscape which has been my classroom.

Every effort has been made to contact the holders of copyright material but if any have been inadvertently overlooked, the publisher will be pleased to make the necessary alterations at the first opportunity.

Order queries: please contact Bookpoint Ltd, 39 Milton Park, Abingdon, Oxon OX14 4TD. Telephone: (44) 01235 400414, Fax: (44) 01235 400454. Lines are open from 9.00–6.00, Monday to Saturday, with a 24-hour message answering service. Email address: orders@bookpoint.co.uk

British Library Cataloguing in Publication Data
A catalogue record for this title is available from The British Library

ISBN 0 340 74316 6

First published 1999
Impression number 10 9 8 7 6 5 4 3 2
Year 2004 2003 2002 2001 2000

Typeset by Transet Limited, Coventry, England.
Printed in Great Britain for Hodder & Stoughton Educational, a division of Hodder Headline plc, 338 Euston Road, London NW1 3BH by Cox and Wyman Limited, Reading, Berks.

CONTENTS

Introduction: A voyage of discovery 1

Chapter 1 The Old Straight Track 3

'A flood of ancestral memory' 3
Laying out the tracks 5
Waymarks and crosses 7
Landmarks 10
Stones – great and small 11
Moving the earth 13
Trees – living landmarks 14
Water – reflecting the way 16
Sacred places 16
Churchyards – survivals of the sacred grove 18
Roads and tracks 18
Place names 19
Ley examples 21

Chapter 2 Ley hunting 26

Mapwork 27
Out into the field 29
Delving into the archives 32
Problems and opportunities 32
Alternative ley hunting 33

Chapter 3 Patterns in the Land 35

Early discoveries 35
The Straight Track Club 36
Landscape geometry 37
The landscape detective 38
The Avalon Society 39
The earliest survey? 39
SCEMB lines 40
Standard distances and cosmic force 40
Decline and revival 41

Chapter 4 Skyways and Landmarks 42

Tony Wedd 42
Leys, flying saucers and magnetic currents 43
The Ley Hunter's Club 46

Chapter 5 The Earth Spirit 48

Earth energy 48
The energy of life 49
The living earth 51
The flow of energy 52
Dowsing 52
Ley dowsing 53

Chapter 6 Earth Lines 58

A worldwide phenomenon 58
The lines of Nazca 59
In the New World 59
Ruling lines 62
Song lines 63
Reaves and cursuses 63
Death roads 63
A corridor of sanctity 64
Ghost roads 66
Fairy paths 66

Chapter 7 Lines of the spirit 68

Consciousness and straightness 68
Spirit paths 70
Shamanic journeying 70
Witch flight paths 71

Chapter 8 The straight debate 74

'They didn't walk in straight lines!' 74
'They weren't all there at the same time!' 75
'It doesn't mean a thing!' 75
'So, what *are* leys?' 78
Meshes and grids? 79
Long-distance leys? 79
Subconscious siting? 80
The cultural context 81

Chapter 9 Straightness and life 84

The ley as an archetype 84
The moon and the apple tree 86
Conclusion 88

Appendix: Waymarks to further study 89

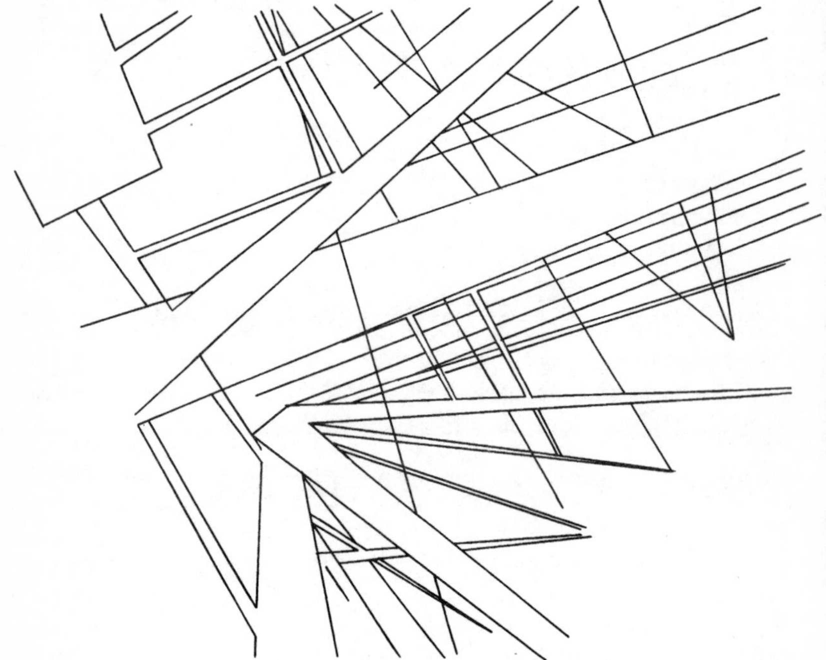

A small part of the extensive landscape lines near Nazca in Peru

INTRODUCTION

A voyage of discovery

Talk of leylines tends to conjure up a certain image – they represent, along with crystal healing, hugging trees and talking to dolphins, everything that comes under the label of 'New Age'. It is no longer unusual, in conversation about anything from an unexplained death to a win on the lottery, for someone to exclaim: 'Well, they lived on a leyline, you know!', as if that settled the matter and rendered any further discussion unnecessary. Leylines have been blamed for just about everything from climatic change to fluctuations in the financial markets without, in most cases, the speaker having other than a very vague idea of what they are talking about.

People sometimes get in touch with me wanting to know 'where the leylines are' in their particular area and can they buy a map charting them. While I can sometimes help with examples that I know about, my reply is usually along the lines of 'Why not go out and look for them yourself?' This isn't meant to be rude: it's more a recognition of the state of the subject. Things are a long way from being cut and dried and it is up to *you* to do the work. I hope this book will give some clues as to what to do and how to go about it.

Some subjects carry such a weight of tradition behind them that several years of study seem to be necessary even to get on to the bottom rung, let alone make an original contribution. Leylines, or 'leys' as they are more simply known, are not like that at all. Their study is relatively new and it is less than 80 years since they were discovered. Many deny their very existence and there is no set body of knowledge as there is in, for example, physics or chemistry.

This state of affairs has, of course, both advantages and drawbacks. The disadvantage is that it has not all been fully worked out and therefore, to a greater degree than in most other subjects, it really *is* up to you to do the work. But the positive side of things is that any one individual can make a real and genuine contribution to the body of knowledge.

This is a living subject because ideas about leys are constantly being developed and enlarged upon. Sometimes, admittedly, there is argument about their meaning and even if they exist at all in the traditional sense.

As that collector of the unconventional, Charles Fort, once said, 'One measures a circle, beginning anywhere'. In other words, it doesn't much matter where we choose to begin in looking into a subject. But I have started with the individual who, above all, is credited with the discovery of leys – Alfred Watkins.

I hope you will take a journey with me through time, forward from the moment when leys were first discovered to the present day. We will pick up ideas as we go along, tracing a story which is still evolving and you will not only get the essential facts about leys, but also become aware of opinions and speculations as well. I will try to make it clear which is which. Above all, it will be a voyage of discovery not just into the hidden corners of the landscape but into the subtle dimensions of our own consciousness.

Practice

What comes into your mind when 'leylines' are mentioned? Think about this and what it is about them that attracts you. (You must have been attracted or you wouldn't have opened this book!)

We are going on a journey and I want you to prepare for it by making sure you pack something and leave something. I want you to bring along an open mind, but also to try and leave behind any preconceived ideas you may have about leylines, for you may be in for some exciting surprises! Both these things are easier said than done, I know! But try to make the attempt!

The Old Straight Track

'A Flood of Ancestral Memory'

Alfred Watkins (1855–1935) – The discoverer of leys [based on a photograph by Major F.C. Tyler]

Thursday 30 June 1921 started out as just another day for 66-year-old Alfred Watkins. He enjoyed his work with the family firm of flour millers; it took him all over his native county of Herefordshire and across the border into Wales. It also gave him the opportunity, as he went on his farm visits, to study the countryside he loved and he was in no hurry to retire.

He had started early and, by late afternoon, he had finished his work for the day. The weather was fine and clear and, rather than go straight home, he decided to have a look at his map for somewhere interesting to explore. He was fascinated by the countryside and its history and, in over 50 years of study, had got to know it well. He was a photographer in an age when taking photographs involved carrying heavy equipment up hills and across fields.

As he looked at the map, he suddenly became aware of several ancient sites which seemed to fall on a straight line that also passed over prominent hilltops. Watkins' son, Allen, in the biography of his father *Alfred Watkins of Hereford* (Garnstone, 1972) takes up the story:

> *Then without any warning it all happened suddenly. His mind was flooded with a rush of images forming one coherent plan. The scales fell from his eyes and he saw that over many long years of prehistory, all trackways were in straight lines marked out by experts on a sighting system. The whole plan of The Old Straight Track stood suddenly revealed.*

Watkins was not the first to have discovered the alignment of ancient sites, but his vision is the one which has caught the popular imagination: it was an idea whose time had come. He later described it as if 'a flood of ancestral memory' had entered his consciousness.

His knowledge and photographs of the Herefordshire countryside stood him in good stead. Within three months he was giving an illustrated talk to the prestigious Woolhope Naturalists' Field Club explaining how prehistoric people had laid out straight trackways across the surface of the English and Welsh countryside using the simplest of surveying equipment and that, after thousands of years, some of these could still be traced. He named them 'leys' as, based on place-name evidence, he believed this was what they had once been called.

He found a few stretches of track which seemed to have survived, but not enough to draw attention in their own right. What drew Watkins to his conclusions was something much more striking, which helped him to understand how and why they were originally laid out. What he found were landmarks – features placed along the way to tell travellers they were 'on track' and going in the right direction.

These landmarks were just the sort of things we might expect the ancient people to have used to mark their tracks: distinctive boulders that could well have been rolled into place to act as primitive 'milestones'; artificial earth mounds and piles of stones positioned on hilltops so that the traveller could see them from a distance; clumps of Scots pines, tall and dark and prominent at all seasons.

After Watkins had told his story to the Woolhope Club, he followed it up with a series of books, the best-known being *The Old Straight Track*, published in 1925 (see Appendix). Readers in many different places found these tracks for themselves so that, today, we know that straight tracks are a worldwide phenomenon.

But to walk in a straight line towards your objective is not always the easiest way of getting there. It is often much less effort, though longer, to walk round a hill than over the top. So, Watkins' assertion that the ancient people laid out straight tracks over hill and dale strikes us as odd, to say the least. Even Watkins did not give a real explanation, except to say that it was difficult for us with our 'civilized mentality' to judge what ancient peoples would have done.

What he did, however, was to describe clearly what he saw. He made a guess at the 'how', but the 'why' was always ultimately beyond him.

Laying out the tracks

Watkins demonstrated convincingly that it was well within the capabilities of ancient people to set out these straight lines accurately across the landscape and that advanced surveying methods were not needed.

How the leys were sighted [from the cover of Watkins' *The Ley Hunter's Manual*]

All that was required were two surveyors, each with a tall straight staff. By sighting over each other's staff to two distant but visible landmarks it was easy enough, by trial and error, to find an intermediate point that was exactly on the line joining the two landmarks. The line could also be extended in the same way. Watkins even claimed that The Long Man of Wilmington – a large ancient figure cut into the chalk of the South Downs and holding two staffs – could actually be a picture of one of these surveyors.

The Welsh border country, where Watkins made his early discoveries, is hilly and he soon realized that all his leys started (or finished) on a hilltop, which would make sense if they were initially laid out in the way he proposed. The highest hill in an area was often chosen, but those which had a distinctive shape, or were otherwise prominent, were also selected. They were sometimes traditional beacon sites or considered holy, or otherwise special, in some way.

Watkins became convinced that long-distance trade was the reason for the tracks' existence. Flints, salt, pottery and other commodities were certainly carried considerable distances in early times, as we know from archaeological evidence. He felt that the purpose of the tracks survived in the place names which existed along them. 'White' names were related to the salt trade; 'red' names to the trade in pottery; and 'cheap' or 'chip' elements indicated that flint traders used the track. This, he felt, had happened so long ago that most traces of the tracks themselves had disappeared – only odd fragments remaining, as if by chance.

What *did* remain, he was convinced, were features placed along the tracks to guide the traveller, by day and by night.

Waymarks and crosses

In ancient times the countryside was much wilder and more wooded than it is now and some form of mark would have been needed to let the traveller know that they were on the path and heading in the right direction.

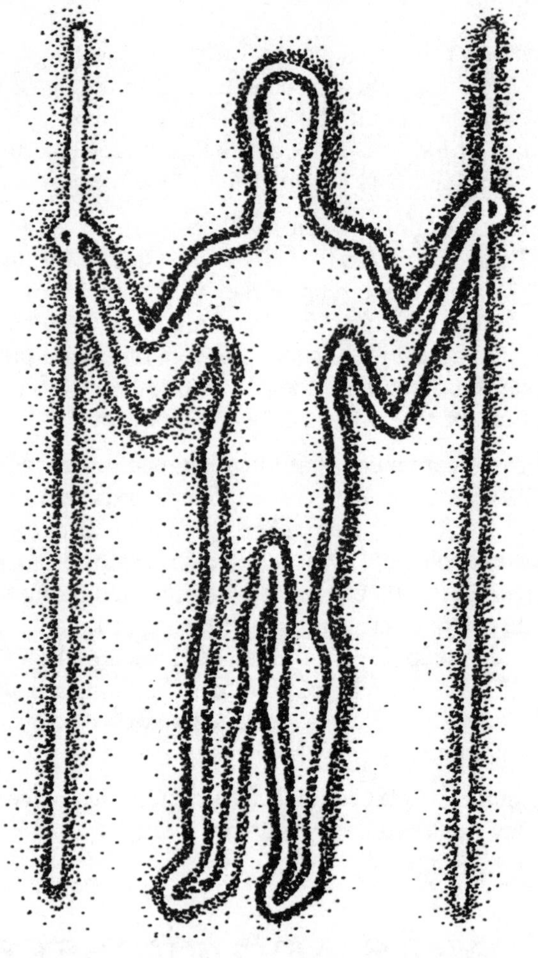

The Long Man of Wilmington – Was this ancient figure cut into the Sussex Downs an image of a ley surveyor with staffs?

What sort of marks were there and where were they located?

The best answer is to imagine walking along a present-day footpath, but without the usual accompaniment of a map. If the footpath is reasonably clear, then the only place you might need a mark is at a junction. If, however, it is overgrown, then confirmation that you are on the right path, or indeed on any path at all, would be useful. If the mark was right beside the track, it need not be anything very large, as long as it was something distinctive and permanent.

In many parts of the country, *markstones* fulfilled this function admirably. They are often rocks known as 'glacial erratics' – boulders picked up by the glaciers of the last Ice Age and deposited at random. To do their job they would have to be small enough for a few people to move them to the nearest ley but large enough to be noticed and perhaps to provide a seat for the weary traveller. Generally, they were left in their original form, with little obvious

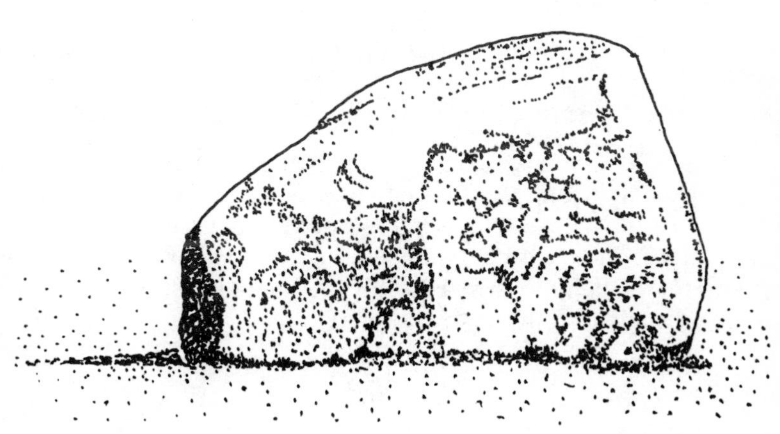

A markstone, Swanland, East Yorkshire

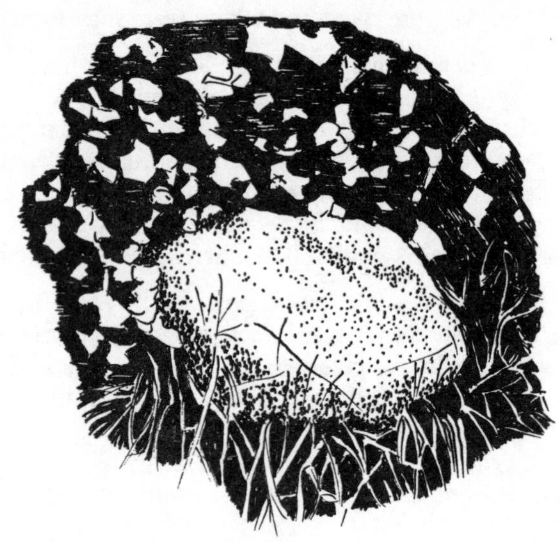

A markstone, Catwick, East Yorkshire

working or shaping. In many ways markstones can be looked on as the forerunners of the milestone and a surprising number can still be found, particularly at road or track junctions and beneath hedges, if you keep your eyes open.

The wayside preaching cross is often merely the Christianization of an earlier stone, either by the simple expedient of carving a cross into it or by forming a socket in the top of the stone and erecting a cross on that. Often the cross-base (the original markstone) is all that now remains.

Landmarks

If you *have* strayed off the path, then what you need is a more distant landmark that you can work towards. This needs to be visible and therefore on a high point and noticeable in some way above the surrounding landscape. Also, for maximum visibility when climbing up the slope from a valley floor, it needs to be on the brow of the hill rather than at the very top. This is just what Watkins, and others since, have found.

The easiest landmark is one which already exists and, as we have seen, Watkins believed the terminal points were initially chosen because they were distinctive in some way, perhaps an unusually shaped or coloured rock, and could be recognized from the valley below.

But these, by their nature, would be rare and would only be initial points anyway. The surveyors could not rely on the intermediate ridges to be marked in any significant or useful way so people would do what they have always done and imitate nature. In a worldwide tradition that also includes the alteration of mountain tops in China to provide better 'feng shui', the ley-makers would create their mark by moving earth and stones until they got what they wanted.

Stones – Great and Small

The tradition of cairn building is probably the earliest example of such alterations to nature, where stones are piled up to form a rough pyramid or cone shape which can be seen for a considerable distance. These are frequently found on the tops or brows of hills and, indeed, it seems a common practice for walkers and climbers to carry a stone up a hill and add it to the pile.

Sometimes one large stone, which has clearly been erected at some stage, marks the horizon. Theoretically, it is difficult to tell the difference between an ancient standing stone and the sort of stone gateposts which are common in certain areas. In practice, this isn't usually a problem. Indeed, the whole matter can be somewhat confused because conveniently located standing stones *were* often later used for gateposts.

The Chiding Stone, Chiddingstone, Kent – A distinctive natural stone outcrop through which several leys pass

Moving the Earth

An elaboration of the cairn and, indeed, a substitution for it on non-rocky ground, is the mound, constructed of, or surfaced with, earth. Mounds may, of course, have had several functions. They *were* used for burial, but many of the more elaborate ones, such as the Neolithic long barrows, may also have served for rituals and for initiatory practices, such as the 'temple sleep', where prophetic dreaming took place at a sacred site. Watkins' contribution was to show that the *location* of these mounds was also significant – a point which has only recently been taken up by the archaeologists.

Willy Howe – a Neolithic Mound on the Yorkshire Wolds. Legends of fairies are associated with this prominent mound, which has at least two leys passing through it. [drawing based on a photograph by the author]

Mounds can be as prominent on the heights as cairns but, in the valleys, Watkins found that there was often a ditch surrounding them which had been filled with water and that the water increased their visibility by reflecting the bright sky.

There are many earthworks up on the hills which have no apparent practical use for defence or stock control but which, nevertheless, are situated in a position which makes them a prominent feature when viewed from below. Watkins noticed that such earthworks, together with the sunken nature of the track itself, sometimes formed a 'notch' on the skyline which was visible only when you were on the right track. He considered this a deliberate and useful feature.

One of the most radical ways in which hilltops can be made distinctive is by actually changing their shape. The 'feng shui' practices in China have become well known but this was also quite common in Britain. However, it has not been generally recognized for what it is because this purpose has been disguised as part of what have variously been called Hill Forts, Camps or Defensive Fortifications.

Basically, people lived on the tops of hills for security and defence and created earthworks to help in this, sometimes very elaborate ones in excess of what was strictly needed. Watkins found that virtually all the camps in Herefordshire were on leys, but these tended to go along the edges rather than through the middle of the camp. Indeed, in some cases, such as at Credenhill, the leys appeared to determine the shape of the camp itself. There also remain some earthworks that seem to have no defensive or other practical function at all.

Trees – Living Landmarks

Watkins found that tree clumps often marked the ley as it crossed over a hill or ridge. Scots pine, which he called 'The Tree of the Ancient Track', was most frequent. Undoubtedly pines made very good markers, being evergreen, much darker than the surrounding vegetation and standing tall of it.

The problem is, of course, that the ley system as proposed by Watkins is claimed to be several thousand years old and individual trees usually live only a few hundred. And yet, Watkins and others

have consistently found well-formed tree clumps exactly on the line. These could not be the original trees (with the possible exception of yews), so we have to conclude that they have regenerated on the same spot, helped perhaps by people who were aware of their significance.

The Scots pine clump played an important part in my own introduction to leys, as you will see later so I have a very soft spot for them, even though Watkins, for obvious reasons, called them 'a weak point for the ley-hunter'!

A Clump of pines at Lyewood Common, Kent. The darkness of the pines and the way they rise above the surrounding vegetation make them good ley mark-points.

Water – Reflecting the way

Water reflects and Watkins noted how rivers and streams, under certain light conditions, showed up clearly when viewed from a high point. He found, on following his leys, how frequently a pond or moated mound, particularly with the older circular form of moat, occurred on them. He surmized that they were intended to be seen from afar in order to guide travellers and even, in some circumstances, to reflect the glow from beacon fires on the hill above.

A Dewpond near Huggate on the Yorkshire Wolds. Ponds are often ley mark-points.

Sacred places

Places that were sacred to the old pagan religions and, in turn, to Christianity, frequently seem to be found on leys and we must conclude from this that they are important as terminal points or perhaps derive their importance from being on the ley itself. Natural places of awe and beauty having special qualities like rock outcrops, caves and springs feature frequently as terminal points, and provide a hint that trade may not have been the sole reason for leys, as we shall see. From very early times, people have built sacred enclosures on leys, such as the vast majority of stone circles.

Castlerigg Stone Circle in Cumbria. There are several significant alignments and orientations to the surrounding mountain peaks.

The mazes or labyrinths to be found cut into the turf of village greens or marked on remote seashores by rounded boulders often turn out to be on leys. They symbolize many things, including life's pilgrimage, and running a maze has long been known as a way of changing one's state of consciousness.

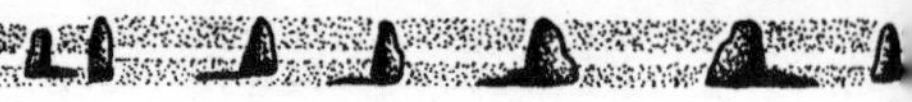

Churchyards – survivals of the sacred grove

Churches also occur frequently on leys or, more accurately, churchyards do. Churches are clearly of too recent origin to have been ley markers, but many are known to have been built on earlier pagan sites, such as Rudston in East Yorkshire, where the tallest standing stone in the country can be found right next to the church. The tower of Cascob church in Wales is actually built on a tumulus, or ancient mound, and there are documentary records showing that Goodmanham church in East Yorkshire is built on the site of a former pagan temple. The church at Knowlton in Dorset stands in the middle of a Neolithic henge.

Following new dating techniques, it now appears that many churchyard yews are far older than the churches themselves (such as those at the villages in Surrey and Sussex both named Crowhurst), which gives rise to the intriguing possibility that some churchyards are actually a continuation of the ancient sacred groves. Certainly in England, many who look for leys on maps find that churches seem to line up readily, and that most leys pass through at least one church and very likely more.

Roads and tracks

England is a densely populated country with a long history – roads and tracks come and go; Watkins likened the countryside to an old man who may have some of his old clothes in the back of the wardrobe but whose baby-clothes will have long since disappeared. In other words, it would be difficult to trace the existence and position of leys purely from present-day roads.

However, he did find some roads and tracks still following leys and certainly they often seem to go through crossroads and points

Rudston Church and Monolith. The Church was built next to the tallest standing stone in Britain.

where three and five lanes end, with amazing frequency. In folklore, crossroads are the scene of much ghostly activity and are the province of the goddess Hecate. Witches and those who had committed suicide were denied burial in the churchyard, but were frequently laid to rest at crossroads, the implication being that such places held a certain sanctity.

Leys also seem to cross rivers at the sites of ancient fords, perhaps not following the alignment of the modern road, but emphasizing that the point of crossing has remained the same even though the paths to it may have changed over the years.

Place Names

A ley which I know in Kent reaches the Greensand Ridge at a place called One Tree Hill. While it no longer exists, such a tree must

have been an important mark to give its name to the place and reminds us that names can provide a clue when the physical marks themselves have disappeared. Of course, place names may have changed considerably since they were first written down and we can only guess at changes further back than that. The English Place-Name Society has produced a volume for each county of England, which gives the likely meanings of village, street, farm, field and other names, including earlier recorded versions.

To start with the word 'ley': Watkins came to believe that this was the name by which the old straight tracks were at one time known. The element 'ley' in a place name is generally thought to indicate meadow-land, and Watkins suggested that this meaning had evolved from 'a clearing in woodland through which a straight track passed' to the word for the track itself. There is additional confirmation in that the French word *layon* means a track used by sportsmen and *laie* means a bridleway or forest ride.

However, because its usual meaning is 'meadow' it is, in practice, better to ignore the element 'ley' when looking for place name evidence. Certainly Watkins, towards the end of his life, stopped using the word, replacing it with the purely descriptive 'old straight track' or the word 'alinement', insisting on that old English spelling rather than the French *alignment* now in common use.

Other place names that Watkins found associated with leys seemed to be related either to the way in which they were constructed or the goods which were carried along them. Thus the elements 'black', 'cole' and 'dod' relate in Watkins' eyes respectively to the original surveyors' beacon fires and their habit of 'dodging' around to fix the line. Earlier we saw how he thought that elements such as 'white', 'red' and 'chip' related to the goods which were carried along these tracks.

Whilst place-name evidence is fraught with difficulties and misinterpretations, it is certainly true that unusual names of unknown origin can occur with surprising frequency 'along the line'.

Ley examples

In his books, Watkins gives many examples of leys, particularly in Herefordshire and the Welsh borders. This countryside is one of prominent hills and valleys and the emphasis which he gives to different ley markers reflects the character of that landscape. Thus we have many hills suitable as terminal points, with cairns, mounds and notches and the occasional Scots pine clump on the ridges, together with hollow ways, fords, moats and ponds on the lower ground. In practice, though, many leys passed through churches and the edges of camps, as in the diagram below of leys to the south-east of Hereford. Watkins' books give many more.

An excellent example of a ley with a number of markers in a short distance is the Saintbury ley in Gloucestershire, discovered by Paul Devereux and Ian Thomson. It has a total length of just 5.6 kilometres (3.5 miles) and runs from the Vale of Evesham up through the village of Saintbury on to the heights of the Cotswolds.

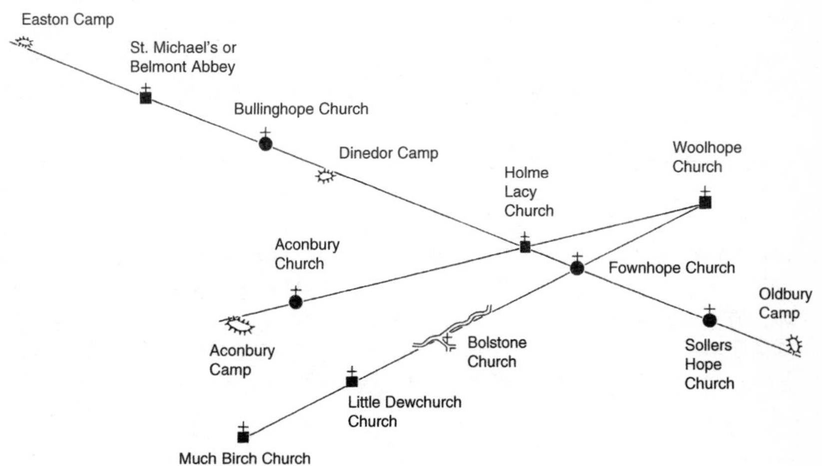

Leys south of Hereford, discovered by Alfred Watkins. Churches and Camps are the main markers.

Swine Church from Sutton Churchyard. The alignment between them passes the ramparts of tree-topped Castle Hill.

The points on the ley include a crossroads with a wayside cross; a length of road leading to Saintbury Church, which houses what is recognized to be a pre-Christian altar; a Bronze Age round barrow; a Neolithic long barrow in the middle of an Iron Age fort and a Saxon pagan cemetery. The ley ends at Seven Wells Farm, an ancient homestead surrounded by a semi-circle of trees: a dramatic site which was the setting for the 1948 novel by historian Hugh Ross Williamson entitled *The Silver Bowl* which was about the survival of witchcraft in the area.

Another example of a ley comes from East Yorkshire and stretches from the outskirts of the city of Hull to the North Sea. It is significant, not just in terms of the mark points, but also their spacing. The ley consists of four churches in exact alignment – Sutton, Swine, Goxhill

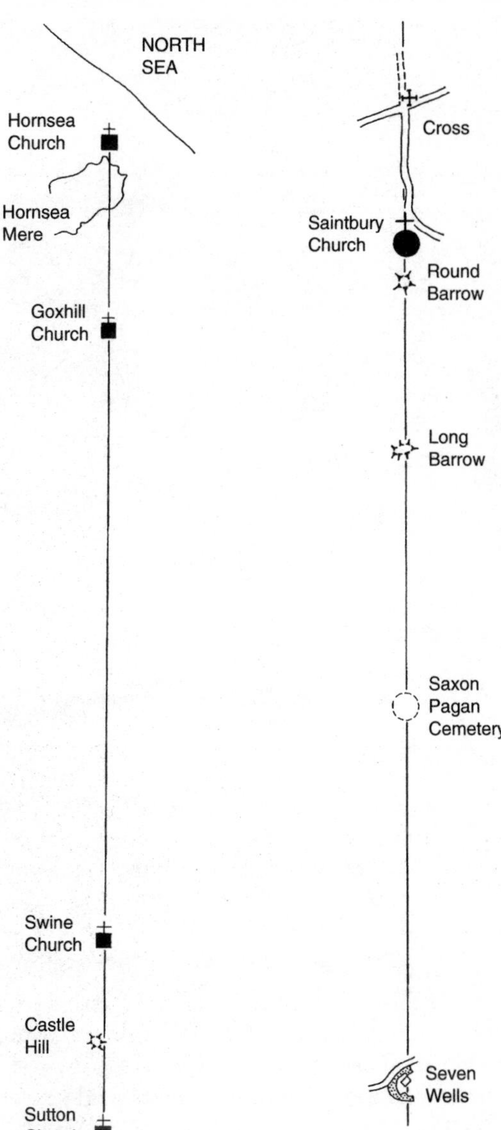

The Sutton – Hornsea Ley,
East Yorkshire

The Saintbury Ley,
Gloucestershire

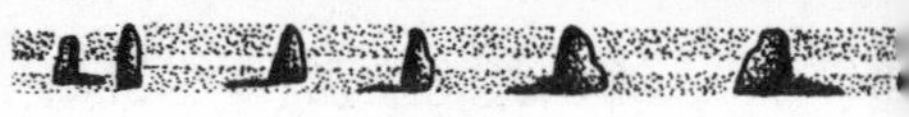

A visual alignment across the Leven Estuary in Morecambe Bay, from the Sunbrick Stone Circle on Birkrigg Common. The line passes over Bardsea Church, through the site of an old chapel on Chapel Island and ends at a prominent clump of trees on Mount Barnard.

and Hornsea. What makes this so special is that the distance between Sutton and Swine churches is exactly the same, 3.2 kilometres (2 miles), as the distance between Goxhill and Hornsea churches. So, it forms a nice geometrical design. Moreover, exactly half-way between Sutton and Swine churches is the mound known as Castle Hill. The line passes over the edge of the ramparts of the mound and there is a local legend that the monks of old had a tunnel from Swine church to Castle Hill, appearing there as ghosts.

The drawing on page 24 shows a very good example of visual alignment. It is a view across the estuary of the River Leven, south of Ulverston, in north-west England. The stones in the foreground of the picture are part of the Sunbrick stone circle on Birkrigg Common. The spire of Bardsea church can be seen touching an island in the middle of the estuary. This is Chapel Island and it has the remains of an ancient chapel exactly on the line, which finishes at a prominent clump of trees on top of a hill called Mount Barnard. This is not a particularly unusual or spectacular ley, but it is unusual in that four landmarks on the line are visible from one spot.

But this line across water hints at something which has become obvious since Watkins' time: leys are far more than just trackways. They lead us in some interesting directions, and I hope you will follow me along them to see just where they are going.

Practice

Get a 1:50,000 scale Ordnance Survey map (or the equivalent) for your local area, in preparation for the exercise in Chapter 2.

A good map is a rich symbol of the landscape and is a good subject for meditation.

But first get to know how to read a map by using the key – the so-called Conventional Signs – and the method of locating a site by means of Grid References.

Then just sit and look at the map and get to know it. See what places you recognise and what places attract you most. Think about why that might be.

Think about the possible meanings of place names and then check them with a local place-name volume. But don't necessarily assume that the book is right and that your intuitions are wrong!

2 Ley Hunting

Whatever the truth behind Watkins' discovery, the idea of leys was one that was both attractive and accessible to all. Here was a brand-new subject that people could not only understand but make a personal contribution towards.

Watkins recognized this and, in *The Old Straight Track,* he included an appendix entitled 'Ley Hunting', which consisted of practical hints to assist readers in finding leys for themselves. Its title now strikes us as being somewhat aggressive and predatory but it has become firmly established. Watkins' *The Ley Hunter's Manual* appeared in 1927 and the journal *The Ley Hunter,* started in 1965, is still with us so, for the moment at least, we are stuck with the term!

The *Birmingham Post,* reviewing one of Watkins' books, called ley hunting 'a new outdoor hobby' and, while for many of us it is somewhat more than the sort of activity that the word 'hobby' conjures up, it certainly takes us outdoors into the countryside.

My aim in this chapter is to give you the basic ideas on how to go about ley hunting. In a sense, it's the ideal way – something to aim at. Don't worry if you find that you have missed some of the steps or want to ignore something. At least you will know how it *should* be done! Like most activities, the main thing is to have a go. You can always improve your technique later.

To set about ley hunting, the three essentials are map work, fieldwork and archive work.

Mapwork

The essential fact about a ley is that it is straight and it follows that it will appear straight when plotted on a map. (In fact, there is an inevitable distortion caused by the fact that a map is a flat representation of the curved surface of the Earth, but over the distances we are working to this can safely be ignored.)

Now, maps vary in quality in different parts of the world but, for the moment, we will concentrate on ley hunting in Britain, which is where Watkins made his initial discoveries. British Ordnance Survey maps are generally recognized to be among the best in the world.

To start with, choose an area which is reasonably near to where you live, because part of ley hunting involves going out and following leys on the ground, and you will progress much faster if you get to know the area you are investigating. There are many things which don't appear even on the largest-scale maps and they can really only be discovered if you go out and look at the line on the ground. These include not just physical features but such things as site intervisibility – whether you can see one point from another – which is important if you are trying to demonstrate the validity of Watkins' theories. Indeed, you can think of Watkins as an inspiration: even though well past retirement age, he walked considerable distances across muddy fields and up mountains carrying his heavy camera because he realized the importance of getting to know the landscape.

First, if you haven't got one already, get a 1:50,000 Ordnance Survey map of your local area. This should preferably be flat, because the folds distort straight lines to some extent. Ideally, you need two copies of the map – a flat one on which you can plot lines accurately and a folded one that you can use in the field. If you find a good line you will probably want to transfer it onto the smaller-scale 1:25,000 map for the area, 4 centimetres to 1 kilometre (about 2.5 inches to 1 mile), which has a lot more detail and makes it easier to check the accuracy of the line.

Look through the list of mark-points that were mentioned in Chapter 1. Not all of them will be marked on maps – tree clumps, markstones and notches, for example, can be found only by going out into the field and having a look for yourself. So, you are left with mounds and cairns (perhaps marked as 'tumuli' on the map), earthworks of various sorts, 'castle' mounds, churches, some standing stones and stone circles, wayside crosses, crossroads and straight lengths of road and track, fords or bridges across rivers and streams and, possibly, beacon sites.

With these in mind, lay the flat map out on a drawing board, table top or other flat area large enough so you can spread it out completely, pinning or weighting it down to stop it rolling up. You also need a long, preferably at least 75 centimetres (30 inch), transparent plastic ruler and a sharp pencil, at least 'H' hardness. A propelling pencil is ideal because it doesn't need sharpening.

Now, play around with the map, the ruler and the pencil as if it were a sort of game. Take a likely point (a stone circle or ancient church, for example), put the tip of the pencil on it and slide the ruler up to it until it just touches it. Then move the ruler round, keeping it up against the pencil and see whether there are any likely mark points which line up, or just move the ruler round at random.

Don't worry about being over-enthusiastic – you'll probably draw lots of lines that, on reflection, turn out not to be leys. It doesn't matter: let your enthusiasm run away with you – for a while, at any rate! The important thing is to enjoy yourself – that is the right frame of mind in which to be inspired: you can sort out the likely lines later.

When you find at least four and preferably five points accurately aligned, draw a pencil line through them. The shorter the total length, the more significant the line is likely to be – four points on a line going the whole length of the map is not really enough. In practice, you will know what feels significant. You are not committing yourself at this stage to saying 'This is a ley'. It is more a case of having some points in alignment that might prove worthy of further investigation on the ground.

Of course, the main feature which characterizes a ley is its straightness and we have seen that it was well within the capabilities of ancient surveyors to achieve that fairly accurately. So, make sure that the points on the map actually *do* line up precisely and discard those alignments which are only approximate. For all practical purposes, the points *must line up*.

Some points, of course, will line up purely by chance. It is not at first very easy to distinguish between these and 'proper' leys, but after a while you will find that leys tend to follow the 'grain' of the landscape as revealed in the map. They will tend to pass through all sorts of confirmatory points, like isolated farmsteads, zig-zags in roads, track junctions and the like – not mark-points in their own right but indicators of something which comes through from the landscape to the map, which is acting as a powerful symbol.

Don't try too hard. Put the map away when you feel you've done enough and then get it out again on another occasion. After 'playing around' for a while you will find that you have plotted quite a few lines. Now is the time to transfer these onto your folded map and select one of the most likely lines which you have found. You are ready to go exploring!

Out into the field

So, how do you choose a likely line? Theoretically it's difficult to say what a likely line is but, in practice, you will know – it will be a line that has a large number of points, but also one which goes through somewhere that means something special to you. This may seem strange, but I have every confidence that you will know which one you have to start with.

Then work out the direction of the line. You can do this by extending it until it cuts the edge of the map and working out the direction, in degrees, clockwise, from north, with a protractor. This can be adjusted to magnetic north by means of the information which is contained in the margin of the map. This direction is important for, with the aid of a prismatic compass, you can work out, if you are on the ley, where it crosses the horizon and whether there are any marks along the line. A pair of binoculars can also be useful.

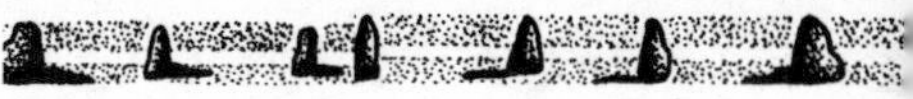

The aim in fieldwork is to follow the line on the ground. This will be so much more revealing than the map. Not only will you spot any waymarks and landmarks that are not on the map, but you will get a feel for the form of the land, and may well feel less tangible things as well, all of which are important to note down.

Be properly equipped when you go out into the field, particularly where the landscape is wild and rough. Waterproof clothing is essential, as are good walking boots. If following a ley by car, a pair of waterproof boots, particularly on farmland in winter, is also recommended.

Remember to act sensibly when you are in the countryside. Follow the **Country Code**:

- Guard against all risk of fire
- Fasten all gates
- Keep dogs under proper control
- Avoid damaging fences, hedges and walls
- Keep to paths across farmland
- Leave no litter
- Safeguard water supplies
- Protect wildlife, wild plants and trees
- Go carefully on country roads
- Respect the life of the countryside

Most of this is just common sense anyway and you will find that, if you treat the land with respect, farmers, landowners and other local people will usually be very interested in what you are doing and may even provide useful information that is relevant to your quest.

Ideally you should walk directly along the line, noting things down as you go. This is rarely practicable, however, where there is enclosed farmland and the best that can be achieved is to take roads and paths in the general direction, stopping at all the points where they cross the line, to see what you can from there.

The best thing is probably to take public transport to a point on the line and then follow it until you can get another bus, train, or whatever, home. Or perhaps someone with a car will drop you off and arrange to meet you later. Those who have difficulty walking can do the same by car, following by public road and stopping each time it crosses the line. This is really second best, but sometimes it is all that can be managed.

The sort of thing to look out for are all the types of mark-point which are not shown on the map and, of course, to examine those that are. It's difficult to be precise about what to look for – really it's anything exactly along the line. You may see a standing stone, a track that isn't marked on the map, or a succession of field gates that are, just by 'coincidence', exactly on the line.

In many ways, winter is a better time to be going ley hunting than summer, for the sun is low and shadows will reveal earthworks that otherwise might be difficult to see. The vegetation is also low, so a hedge-bottom markstone, that might be quite hidden by summer undergrowth, can be seen. However it is also a lot muddier, so don't forget those boots!

Remember the way in which Watkins believed the leys were set out and the purpose of the mark-points as landmarks and waymarks. You should, therefore, note the 'lie of the land' and where your line goes over high ground. See if there is a previously unrecorded mound on the brow of the hill, a skyline notch or perhaps a prominent tree-clump or scatter of pines. Conversely, where your line crosses a river or stream, see if there is any evidence of old hollow-ways leading down to a ford. Or there may be a dammed section of the stream to provide a reflecting pool to guide the traveller.

You will know when something catches your eye. Surprisingly often there are minor features which fall on the line, such as unusual earthworks, a striking tree, a pond or a stone. The thing to do is to note down everything which seems interesting at the time – a sort of 'ley hunting diary'. Note down the date and the weather conditions. Do a sketch map showing the positions and Grid References of all the features which you find and sketches of them, even if these are simple ones.

Better still, take photographs! Watkins was a pioneer photographer and the photographs of ley mark-points which illustrate his books are striking. He found, from experience, that photographs taken 'along the ley' were often better composed and he recommended doing this.

Finally, don't forget your own feelings. There is quite a lot of evidence that leys are not just physical features but may have subtler aspects to them which we will be examining later in the book. So record your impressions, thoughts, emotions and physical feelings at various points along the line: they may be valuable later.

Delving into the archives

To complete your investigations, you really need to look at the wealth of information which is available in your local library or museum.

The Sites and Monuments Record is a list of archaeological sites, including those found by aerial photography. Some of the sites may fall exactly on your line. They may also have legends or folklore attached to them which are contained in books or magazine articles which the library may possess.

Of course, in a rapidly changing landscape, many features are disappearing and it is here that older maps, such as the first editions of the 6 inches to 1 mile (9.5 centimetres to 1 kilometre) and 25 inches to 1 mile (40 centimetres to 1 kilometre), can be valuable, as they show the positions of features which have now vanished, but which may be referred to in older local history books or journals.

After you have found your ley, walked and researched it and photographed some of the features, why not write it up into an article? There are several regional Earth Mysteries magazines which are on the look-out for well-researched reports of this kind and there are often locally produced magazines devoted to countryside customs and the like which may well be interested.

Problems and opportunities

The old straight tracks occur in many different parts of the world, as we shall see in Chapter 6. Finding them involves essentially the

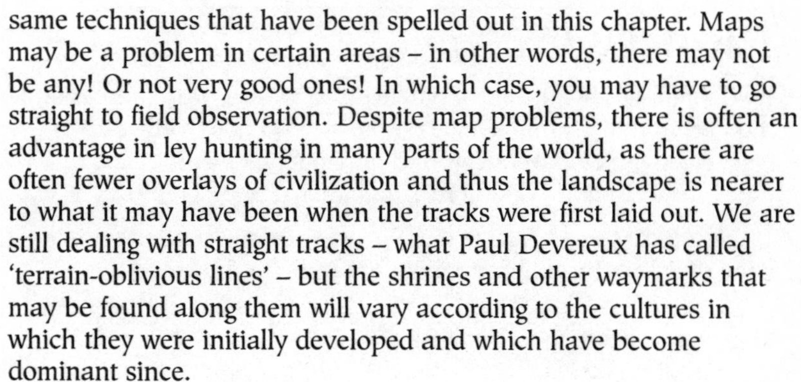

same techniques that have been spelled out in this chapter. Maps may be a problem in certain areas – in other words, there may not be any! Or not very good ones! In which case, you may have to go straight to field observation. Despite map problems, there is often an advantage in ley hunting in many parts of the world, as there are often fewer overlays of civilization and thus the landscape is nearer to what it may have been when the tracks were first laid out. We are still dealing with straight tracks – what Paul Devereux has called 'terrain-oblivious lines' – but the shrines and other waymarks that may be found along them will vary according to the cultures in which they were initially developed and which have become dominant since.

Alternative Ley Hunting

I have stressed the importance of getting out into the landscape to look at leys on the ground, but I do appreciate that, for many, this will not be possible for a variety of reasons, including disability. Even so, it is still possible to go ley hunting, but it is a journey of the mind or what has been called astral travel or out-of-body experiencing.

After you have found a likely line on the map, sit looking at the map and meditate on it, trying to visualize the landscape. Do this just before you go to sleep at night and then remember to record your dreams the following morning. If things go right you may well find that, after a few days, you will start to remember rather strange dreams where you actually feel as if you are flying or moving along the line. Record what you experienced and saw. This links up with some of the most ancient experiences of straightness in the landscape, as we shall see in Chapter 7.

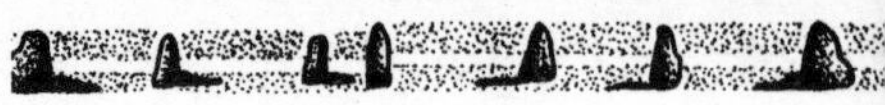

Practice

By definition, ley hunting is practical, so re–read this chapter and then try to find a promising ley on your map, following it up as closely as you can on the ground, making notes at the time of the features that you find, preferably taking photographs as well.

Don't forget to see whether there is any folklore or other written details in your local library about the sites on the ley.

Then write it all up for your 'ley-hunting diary' or for possible publication.

3 Patterns in the Land

Early Discoveries

I mentioned in Chapter 1 that Watkins was not the first to discover alignments of ancient sites. In fact, he was only one in a long line of early observers of linearity in the landscape.

He may well have heard of the work of G.H. Piper, who noticed an alignment of sites in Herefordshire back in the 1880s. Even further back, starting in the 1820s, W.H. Black had been propounding his theory that 'grand geometrical lines' had been laid out in ancient times.

The work of other writers has also been unearthed. In the 1840s the Reverend Edward Duke found alignments between prehistoric sites on Salisbury Plain. Joseph Houghton Spencer, in the 1880s, plotted what, to all intents and purposes, we would today call leys and thought they were the remains of a network of signal stations.

The early knowledge of the orientation of Stonehenge to the midsummer sunrise was expanded on by Norman Lockyer at the turn of the twentieth century when he found alignments linking Stonehenge with other prominent earthworks in the Salisbury Plain area. His ideas were taken up by a group of researchers in Germany in the 1920s and 1930s, including Albrecht, Heinsch and Teudt, who found a whole network of alignments, passing through 'holy hills', beacon sites and 'watchtowers' and oriented on sun and moon rise points.

Watkins may not have been the first to observe straight lines in the landscape and he was by no means the last, but he is the one who,

in some way, captured the public imagination and will always be remembered for his discovery of leys. Indeed, the late Mansfield Forbes, Fellow of Clare College, Cambridge, once remarked to Watkins' son, Allen: 'Your father's name will live for ever.' And it was Watkins whose work gained the greatest circulation and in time sparked off the revival of interest in landscape lines in the 1960s.

Leys really came to public attention when the nationally known firm, Methuen, published what has been called Watkins' 'magnum opus' – *The Old Straight Track* – on 29 October 1925. This book describes Watkins' discoveries at length, including detailed discussion of how he thought leys were set out, the various mark-points involved and the cultural context in which they were placed. It was also profusely illustrated with Watkins' own photographs.

The Straight Track Club

Almost immediately following publication, readers of the book began to find lines in their own area and, naturally, wrote to Watkins to tell him of their discoveries. Such was the interest that the following year, at the suggestion of one of these readers, Barbara Carbonell, Watkins founded what he called The Straight Track Club.

This had a rather interesting means of communication, known as 'postal folios'. A member would write an article about a ley they had discovered or put forward ideas and speculations and send it on to the next member on the list who would add their own contribution, perhaps also making comments on the first member's ideas. And so on, down the list. Over the 22 years of the Straight Track Club's existence, quite a large number of these folios accumulated and they are now housed in Hereford City Library. The Club also had an annual Summer Field Meeting where a local member would guide them to places of interest.

Ley hunting was a new subject and this meant that each individual could make a real contribution, including, of course, both research and speculation on what these lines in the landscape were all about. Looking through the wealth of material contained in the folios it is clear, not only that leys similar to those which Watkins described could be found in all parts of Britain and beyond, but also that not all members accepted without question Watkins' conviction that they were traders' tracks.

Many had doubts because of the sort of landscape the lines went across – up cliffs, across marshes, etc. – and because there were often several closely parallel to each other within a very short distance, which would be superfluous for trackways. Also, members began to find patterns, involving centres where several leys seemed to cross, often where nothing was visible on the map or on the ground, and no obvious reason for them to do so.

Landscape geometry

Ever since it was noted in the eighteenth century that Stonehenge was aligned to the midsummer sunrise, stone circles and other ancient sites had been looked at for possible orientation to significant solar events, particularly midwinter and midsummer sunrise and sunset, Beltane and Lammas sunrise and sunset, as well as to the cardinal points – due north, south, east and west. The 18-year cycle of the moon, and its major and minor north and south standstills (both rising and setting), was also examined for possible correlation. The brightest stars were, of course, also considered. With so many points to choose from, it is not surprising that significant orientations were found. But which were deliberate and which were, in the normal course of things, pure chance, was difficult to determine.

Leys also seemed to be linked into this picture and, it was noted by members of the Straight Track Club and others, that some leys were oriented in the same significant directions to marked points on the horizon. Prominent among these was retired Army officer, Major F.C. Tyler, who presented a challenge to the 'trackway' theory in a book published posthumously in 1939 entitled *The Geometrical Arrangement of Ancient Sites*.

Tyler saw the lines purely as some sort of grand geometrical exercise. His major discovery was that sites appeared to be arranged along

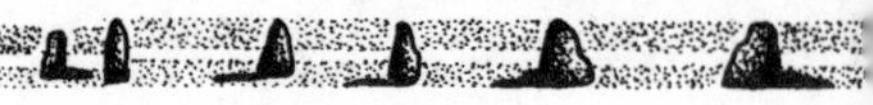

concentric circles, centred not just on prominent places such as Stonehenge but also obscure centres like Wooburn in Buckinghamshire and Churchingford in Somerset. Now, if these patterns had any form of physical reality on the ground, then we are clearly dealing with a culture which, for whatever reason, was concerned with far more than trade and enjoyed making patterns on a gigantic scale. Tyler makes no suggestion as to why these patterns were created, except to propose that they were connected with 'Religious Worship'.

The Landscape Detective

The 1930s was a period when townspeople were becoming more fascinated than ever with the countryside and were using the motor car as well as public transport to take them to where they could walk and explore.

Donald Maxwell was a writer who was very good at enthusing his readers with what he called 'landscape clues' and encouraging them to go out and solve mysteries. It was an approach which Vita Sackville West described as 'a new sort of game' and in recent years it has become a very popular approach to landscape history.

Maxwell's books *A Detective in Essex, A Detective in Sussex, A Detective in Kent* and *A Detective in Surrey* were all published in the early 1930s. Certainly by the time he wrote *A Detective in Surrey* Maxwell had read Watkins and introduced ley hunting as one of his outdoor activities. The book is subtitled 'Landscape Clues to Invisible Roads' and is a dramatized account of how the main characters encounter a 'Watkinsian' who draws their attention away from Roman roads and enlightens them on the subject of leys. They all immediately set to and become enthusiastic ley hunters. All Maxwell's books are great fun to read and evocative of the period between the wars.

The Avalon Society

The onset of war in 1939 brought an end to the Straight Track Club's Summer Meetings and to the postal circulation of members' articles. Indeed, it brought some concern as to whether the Club would survive, as the members were fairly elderly even in its heyday. Indeed, after the Second World War, there was no one to keep the Club going and it folded.

Interest was kept alive during the immediate post-war period through the efforts of Egerton Sykes. He had been a member of the Straight Track Club before the war and was a prolific writer and researcher on topics such as world mythology and Atlantis. In 1946 he formed the Avalon Society which, as well as taking an interest in Arthurian legend and Druidic survivals, was also involved with the ley theory as it supported his own ideas about prehistory.

The Earliest Survey?

One prominent member of the Avalon Society was Kenneth Koop. He had been a surveyor with the Royal Engineers during the Second World War and wrote a paper which was really a logical extension of Tyler's ideas. While his inspiration was clearly derived from Watkins and the Straight Track Club he developed his own system of finding alignments, based on the idea that they may have been some form of early survey. In his paper, *The Earliest Survey?*, first published in 1945, he wrote about a network of lines originating from survey sites which could be identified by place-names, such as Coldharbour, Beggar's Bush and Mount Skippett. He had observed that 'trig. points' – those concrete pillars which the Ordnance Survey had erected in connection with their mapping work – were often positioned close to such sites, which for him helped to confirm his theory, since the same sites would always be attractive to surveyors. But these lines which, as he admitted, were largely based on mapwork, were not leys in the classic Watkins sense and, indeed,

Koop always referred to them simply as 'alignments' and even coined the word 'alignmentology' for their study!

SCEMB LINES

John G. Williams, of Abergavenny in Wales, was working along parallel but separate lines to Watkins. Working primarily in the Black Mountains and other Welsh hills he found what he called SCEMB lines, the letters standing for:

S – standing stones, stone circles
C – cairns or tumuli, camps of pre-Roman origin
E – earthworks of pre-Roman origin
M – moats and mounds of pre-Roman origin
B – burial barrows

These were the only mark-points he would allow, but in the particular area he was studying this limitation still provided enough material for some good alignments, and ones which, moreover, had points of roughly similar age.

STANDARD DISTANCES AND COSMIC FORCE

In 1938, in another development of the 'landscape geometry' ideas, and one which looked forward to the 1960s, Straight Track Club member, Arthur Lawton, found certain standard distances between sites on Beaulieu Heath in Hampshire. Plotting tumuli (ancient mounds), fords, cross–roads and churches, he found the distance of 5702 feet (1738 metres) occurring with amazing frequency. He suggested the existence of a 'cosmic force' which could be detected by dowsers (see Chapter 5) and that its distributionon the surface of the Earth had resulted in certain sites having desirable qualities not found elsewhere.

DECLINE AND REVIVAL

By the early 1960s interest was fading again, and the Avalon Society had become moribund. But interest was about to revive in a remarkable way, largely through the work of one man – Tony Wedd.

PRACTICE

Have a look on a map at some of the leys which you have found in your area.

Think about how well the various ideas – traders' tracks, landscape patterns, an early survey – fit the lines which you have found. What might make you decide which is the most likely?

Think also about other ideas about leys that you may have heard of. What do you think about them? Or do you have your own ideas as to what they might be?

4 Skyways and Landmarks

Tony Wedd

Tony Wedd (1919–1980). The first person to link leys with UFOs.

Tony Wedd was a remarkable person. Brought up in the 1920s and '30s on the edge of the Glastonbury Zodiac, he was conscious of his psychic abilities from an early age and was introduced to leys by a 'chance' meeting with Harold Fletcher Trew, one of the Straight Track

Club members, while out walking one day in the Somerset countryside. Wedd was undoubtedly psychic and, during his time in the Royal Air Force, became skilled in hypnosis. He was interested in the unconventional in life and it was whilst living in London in 1949 that he read *The Old Straight Track* and had his enthusiasm aroused by finding a possible ley through the Scots pine topped tumulus on Hampstead Heath.

In view of his interest in the unconventional, it was hardly surprising that about the time he moved to Kent in 1955 the subject of UFOs (or, as he liked to call them, flying saucers) attracted his attention. He was particularly interested in people who had claimed contact with inhabitants of other planets (the so–called contactees) and he founded an organization called the STAR Fellowship to promote that interest.

One of Wedd's strengths was that he had the ability to see connections between things which others had not noticed. So when Aimé Michel's work, *Flying Saucers and the Straight Line Mystery* (which appeared in 1958), postulated that UFO sightings for any one day, when plotted on a map, fell into straight lines, it set him thinking – 'An alignment of points across the countryside? I've heard of that before!' And he remembered the book he had read while living in Hampstead.

Leys, Flying Saucers and Magnetic Currents

The turning point, or visionary realization, came on re–reading contactee Buck Nelson's book, *My Trip to Mars, The Moon and Venus*. Once sentence stood out: 'The Space People tell me that the places where magnetic currents cross is comparable to a crossroads sign.'

Wedd pondered on the information in these two books – one suggesting an alignment of UFO sightings across the countryside, the other suggesting a physical mark where the 'magnetic currents' used by the saucers crossed each other.

It was at this point that he made the creative leap connecting the two subjects of leys and flying saucers, by speculating that the marks that the saucers used in the landscape were none other than the points that marked the leys. It all fell together in his mind – Watkins' leys and the 'magnetic' currents along which Buck Nelson claimed the saucers travelled were the same thing, but approached from totally different directions.

This certainly gave Wedd a new reason to go out into the countryside around his home looking for landmarks that might indicate the position of the 'magnetic' currents used by the flying saucers. The particular features which he found more than any other on these lines were tree clumps, particularly Scots pines.

His first clue was a good one. A lady living in the small village of Mark Beech saw and reported a pulsating white light moving in a northerly direction. What particularly interested him was the name of the village and that there is a very prominent hilltop clump of mixed trees, including both beech and Scots pine, which can be seen from ridges to north and south. The UFO seemed to be moving along a line which he had already plotted through the clump.

Probably because this sighting so clearly drew attention to a hilltop tree clump; because his first ley hunting encounter back in Hampstead had been with a Scots pine clump; and because there were some very striking Scots pine clumps in the Kent/Sussex border area where he lived, he seemed to focus on these somewhat to the exclusion of other traditional ley marker-points.

But these were located in just the sorts of positions which Watkins had drawn attention to – on hilltops or on a slope so that they could be seen from a valley bottom, and Wedd found strong evidence that these clumps were aligned. Indeed, it was not long before he had plotted a series of parallel lines and related them to other UFO sightings. In 1961, he produced a simple but influential booklet entitled *Skyways and Landmarks* which set out his discoveries and ideas.

Following on from Buck Nelson's use of the term, Wedd used the words 'magnetic current' to describe what it was that the leys were marking. Having discussed it with him at great length, I don't think for one moment that he used the term to indicate that the lines were

Gill's Lap Scots Pine Clump, Ashdown Forest, Sussex.

magnetic in the orthodox sense of the word: clearly they were not. What he intended to put over, and what I think he believed, is that there were certain currents of 'energy' of some sort (without defining it at all closely) which flowed through the atmosphere and across the surface of the Earth, which could be used as a motive force by space ships from elsewhere and that they were helped in finding these currents by visually locating the tree clumps in the landscape below.

He gave as an illustration of this changeover from one 'magnetic' current to another the example of cases in France which Aimé Michel had investigated which involved a UFO travelling in a particular direction, then carrying out a 'falling leaf' manoeuvre, then moving off again in a different direction.

Wedd was quite prepared to follow these ideas through. He met and got information from those who claimed to be in contact with the Space People, including the musician, Philip Rodgers. He also tried to communicate with them himself telepathically. One of his main interests was in trying to make practical use of what he called 'free

energy' – the energy which flowed along the 'magnetic' currents – and made several devices using this principle, including the *roswinga*, or foot-warming soles, which seemed to work and which were to have been made up into *Wenceslas Boots*; and *Coffoostyn*, the Cosmic Coffee Pot, which he never did get to work!

The Ley Hunter's Club

I first heard about leys through meeting Tony Wedd at the STAR Fellowship rally in 1961. Immediately on returning home, I ordered *The Old Straight Track* from the library and read it avidly. I was fascinated, as was a school friend, Jimmy Goddard. We decided to join the Straight Track Club and were most disappointed to learn that it had folded some 13 years previously. We determined to revive it, under the name 'The Ley Hunter's Club'.

I started by making contact with some of the original Straight Track Club members, including Egerton Sykes and Allen Watkins, Alfred's son, who gave us much encouragement and who agreed to become the Club's President. I visited some of the other surviving members, who were all pleased that something was being done to revive interest. We had meetings and field trips and the impressive, but impractical, idea of compiling a National Ley Index. But, because of other commitments, the Club gradually faded away.

One legacy of the Club *did* survive, however. In 1963, we started a bulletin which, in April 1965, became *The Ley Hunter*. Over a third of a century later, this is still going strong. It has been at the forefront of ideas, theories, research and speculation about leys as they changed, developed and interweaved over the years, and it is largely through the pages of *The Ley Hunter* that we can watch the story unfold.

Whether the connection between leys and UFOs is ultimately found to be real or imaginary is only of secondary importance, for it was through becoming aware of Tony Wedd's ideas and reading *Skyways and Landmarks* that many, including myself, who were to spark off the 1960s revival, first heard about leys. The thing to note is that such people as Jimmy Goddard and, through him, John Michell, began to publicize Watkins' ideas to a new generation, and the people who initially heard about leys in this way were the UFO enthusiasts. Naturally, therefore, leys were accepted as having some connection with UFOs and the link was a belief in some sort of energy which flowed along the leys and which powered the UFOs, which were seen as being craft from other planets. The fact is that it was because people like Tony Wedd, Jimmy Goddard and myself thought that there was a connection that interest in leys began to revive. Alongside this, the idea that there may be some 'energy' component to leys began to gain currency.

PRACTICE

See if you can find out where UFOs have been sighted in your area. Your local library may well have a file of press cuttings to help you with this, or there may be a local UFO investigation group.

Where their positions can be determined, plot these sightings on a map, taking care to note the direction of movement, if any.

Now look and see if there appears to be any link between these sightings and the leys you have already plotted. Do the UFOs appear on or near leys? If so, do they appear to move *along* the ley? Or do they seem to be attracted to particular sites? If so, why do you think this might be?

Try to read a book about UFOs and think about the various explanations which have been given. What do *you* think UFOs are? Or are they more than one thing?

5 The Earth Spirit

Earth Energy

As I studied both leys and UFOs, I became convinced that leys were something more than trackways and that there was an 'added ingredient', one which has come to be called 'earth energy' as well as a variety of other names.

I remember vividly the first time I experienced this, when a former editor of *The Ley Hunter*, Paul Screeton, and his wife Pauline took me to the village of Hart in County Durham. There was a large old stone by the roadside. I felt it, and it *tingled*. This (and I have since experienced it many times on other stones) was *real* and it was *strong*.

Another outstanding place that I will always remember is the crypt below the church of Lastingham on the edge of the Yorkshire Moors, which is a powerful example of the way in which this energy can be concentrated by physical form. It is partly cut out of the solid rock and is certainly on at least two leys. To be there alone for even a few minutes will tell you more about earth energy than a whole month of reading. I took Paul Screeton there to experience it and he later wrote that it would 'change your life'.

This energy has been described in folklore as the 'dragon' or 'serpent' power, which seems to have the ability to accumulate in certain stones. It is also present in water, trees, hilltops and certain other special places.

But landscape lines had been linked with some form of earth energy many years before Tony Wedd announced his own ideas. We have

The Merry Maidens, Cornwall. Animals are often sensitive to the earth energies.

already noted how Straight Track Club member Arthur Lawton had suggested that the distribution of a cosmic force on the Earth's surface could be detected and made use of. One of the earliest to write about it was the occultist, Dion Fortune who, in her novel, *The Goat Foot God* (1936), described what she called 'power centres' and 'lines of force' running between them, on which the Old Gods were worshipped. This was put forward in a fictional context, but there was a truth behind it – a seed which was destined to grow.

The Energy of Life

It is an established principle of most ancient religions and philosophies that the whole Universe is essentially one and that every part of it is at some level connected with every other part. As Teilhard de Chardin put it – 'every cubic centimetre is shot through with all that is'. It is enshrined in the holographic plate and is the Hermetic principle of 'as above, so below'. It is, of course, reflected in the findings of

modern physics. Yet it is clear to us in our ordinary everyday reality that things are separate, though the very use of a term like 'ordinary everyday reality' presupposes the existence of other states of being that are in some way 'extra-ordinary'. Recognition of this lies behind many beliefs which accept other states of being, 'vibrations', 'levels' or 'spiritual planes', call them what you will, and acknowledge the existence of that part of us which survives physical death and can be reborn.

Such awareness has been a constant theme in virtually all methods of healing and self-development from ancient times. Sensitives have recognized the existence of bodies more subtle than the physical, interweaving with each other. They have seen them as being composed of flows of energy, which often extend outside the physical body and are perceptible as the aura around human beings, trees and other living things.

The existence of an energy present in all living beings has been recognized since ancient times – the Chinese *ch'i*, the *prana* of the yogis, the *mana* of the kahunas of Hawaii, the *wouivre* of the inhabitants of Brittany and the *munia* of the mediaeval alchemists were all names under which this energy has been known. In more recent times, psychotherapist Wilhelm Reich called it *orgone* and carried out experiments which demonstrated its existence.

This energy flows along meridians, or channels in the body, and is transformed in centres or vortexes of energy, known in Sanskrit as *chakras*, which correspond to the endocrine glands in the physical body. These energy flows are the basis for many systems of healing, including acupuncture, shiatsu, reiki and many others. It is used by healers in dissolving blockages and is brought into adjustment by such practices as chakric balancing.

Reich and, subsequently, others found that this energy obeys certain laws, being concentrated not just in living beings but also in certain specific locations in the landscape.

The Living Earth

In recent times, we have again come to recognize that the whole Earth is a living being in its own right, known to the ancient Greeks as the Goddess Gaia and that we, along with all other beings, are a part of her. This has profound implications for how we see ourselves and how we live, but for our present purposes its importance lies in our perception of the landscape. If the Earth is indeed a living being, then it follows that she too will have a subtle body, with an aura, and the equivalent of chakras and energy flows operating within the landscape itself.

If we take this visionary idea of the Earth as a living being seriously, then it is quite reasonable to assume that the surface of the Earth is alive with energy, flowing along lines and spiralling around vortexes – energy which pulsates, moves, increases and dies away: in other words, the energy of a living being – life energy.

John Michell has called it *The Earth Spirit*, in his 1975 book of that name (see Appendix):

> *Rocks, trees, mountains, wells and springs were recognized as receptacles for spirit, displaying in season their various properties, fertilizing, therapeutic and oracular ... Characteristic of the earth spirit, and in accordance with its feminine nature, is its tendency to withdraw, to decline within the Earth's dark recesses.*

The whole picture which comes across here is of something elusive, something which comes and goes according to its own cycles, something which slips away from those who search for it from the point of view of scientific analysis, but which comes in abundance to those who approach it in the spirit of humility and respect.

For we have to recognize that we are dealing with a *living being* – one who is aware of our presence and who visits us as a matter of grace rather than in accordance with the strict laws of apparent logic.

The Flow of Energy

The archaeologist, Tom Lethbridge, developed a theory which stated that places which showed concentration of what he called the Earth's force-field were just the locations where human emotions could be 'fixed' to the place and that sensitives could pick this up, perhaps much later. So places like waterfalls, springs and hilltop tree clumps would naturally have tales of ghosts attached to them.

Others have found that these same centres of the Earth Spirit have drawn legends and folklore about the presence of fairies and other elemental beings to them, and it is clear that these are locations where the veil between this world and the beyond is thinnest.

But if the Earth is a living being, then these centres are not isolated from each other but connected: the energy must flow between them. Many people have concluded that leys are simply our attempt to mark this flow of energy in straight lines across the landscape.

Now, if this is true, it brings an additional factor into traditional ley hunting. As well as the landmarks, waymarks and lengths of surviving track, the ley could potentially be found by detecting flows of the Earth Spirit.

With the growing interest in parts of the world where traditional 'Watkins-type' leys appear to be rare, particularly in the United States, the primary definition of a ley as an energy line began to be accepted and, as a result, the great tools in finding them were no longer map, compass and boots, but dowsing rods.

Dowsing

Water divining has been known for centuries, often using the forked hazel twig. No one knows quite *how* it works, even though there are all sorts of theories, but the attitude of the technologist or craft-worker is that this is only of secondary importance: the fact that it *does* work is all that really matters! This is why water engineers often use a pair of dowsing rods (a recent version of the cut hazel twig) to locate buried water pipes, because it works and is easier than to use inadequate plans and digging a series of trial pits.

The traditional method is simple. The diviner takes a forked hazel twig, holding it by the forks in a state of what is known as 'unstable equilibrium' so that a very slight movement of the hands will cause the rod to dip or rise considerably. They then walk slowly over an area where it is suspected that water might be found. When the diviner is directly above the water, the rod will move suddenly, apparently of its own accord. What is probably happening is that there is part of us (and our bodies are mostly water anyway) that is sensitive to water in the vicinity and that this moves the muscles in the hands and thus the rod.

Dowsing is the name by which this technique is now generally known. It is clear that this is no orthodox system currently explainable by science, however, since other things can be found in the same way, including lost objects and minerals. Moreover, they can be found just as readily by dowsing a map of the area as by being physically present. We seem to be dealing with something that operates at a level where the unity of all existence is not only experienced but can be used for practical purposes.

Ley dowsing

So, at some stage, it was probably inevitable that someone would use dowsing to try to find a ley.

The technique is essentially the same as that for finding water. Hold a forked twig or a pair of dowsing rods. Walk slowly along a line where you suspect that there is a ley crossing. When the twig dips or rises, or the rods cross, there is the ley.

This can be a valuable adjunct to the methods of ley hunting which I outlined earlier. However, it has also been used to find 'earth energy'. Now, I have no doubt that such energy exists, as I have already described, but there is a real problem in attempting to detect

it with dowsing rods because we don't know that much about it and therefore we can't define it closely.

First of all, what are you trying to find? To answer 'a ley' is not really adequate. We know, for example, what water is or what minerals of various descriptions are. If we are trying to find a lost ring we usually have a pretty clear idea of what we are looking for. But when it comes to leys we've already seen that, from Watkins onwards, there have been many different types of landscape feature that have been called 'leys' or 'leylines'.

The problem is that dowsing will pick up many different things. It is like a radio receiver with a potentially very wide waveband. Take an original alignment of sites such as Watkins found, which may have had a trackway following it. People may have walked such an ancient path for generations and even where it no longer exists it can certainly be detected by dowsing.

But it is all too easy to pick up all sorts of extraneous things including what the dowsers who came here last week thought they were picking up! There is quite a lot of evidence that thought forms of this sort *can* influence a dowser. This is a particular problem at some of the well–known sites which attract a lot of visitors and is akin to the 'interference' which one gets when not quite tuned in to a particular radio station. I am not saying that dowsing doesn't work: just that it isn't necessarily an easy option!

Certain popular viewpoints have a notice erected saying 'Take Your Photographs From Here!'. While this hints at the worst excesses of 'planned tourism', there is a truth that views from certain points are better arranged or composed than others and that these have been chosen by generations of landscape painters and, more recently, photographers. Indeed, it is always a thrill to stand in the footsteps of, say, Alfred Watkins when he took his famous photographs.

Now, dowsers and other sensitives will tell you that they can detect where someone has walked and that old roads and tracks can make their presence felt quite strongly. So, is it beyond the bounds of possibility to suggest that each time someone goes to a viewpoint and admires the view, perhaps looking towards a church with a prominent spire in the middle distance, that such a 'line of sight' could be impressed into the land, repeated hundreds of times over the years and then picked up later by someone dowsing for leys? Certainly Sir George Trevelyan has drawn our attention to the phenomenon of 'active seeing' by using the 'eye beam' to 'feel' a building at a distance and it is generally recognized, by psychics, that there *are* emanations from the eyes.

So, in view of all this, should we give up completely? No! There is definitely a way through!

The clue to successful dowsing seems to be to 'tune in' to whatever it is you want to pick up. In other words, it is not just an automatic process that could be done by a machine. The human component is vital and the dowsing rods or twig are merely extensions of your own mental processes, and you need to hold in your mind as vivid a picture as you can of what you want to find.

But, with all the different ideas about leys, what image can we visualize?

To start with, there is the classic 'Watkins–type' ley. It is likely (and I would usually advise it) that you have already found an alignment by other means, such as map and fieldwork and are trying to track down its exact line. This is relatively straightforward, and a traverse with dowsing rods should fairly quickly give you its position.

On the other hand you might be wanting to detect what has been called 'the Earth's nervous system' and find out how it relates to the landscape in your area. We have called it 'The Earth Spirit' or 'earth energy', but we really still know very little about it. In this case, you might start by visualizing the Earth Goddess Gaia, really feeling her and not just intellectualizing. Feel her as alive, with spirit, energy, life-force, or whatever word you want to use, flowing in and around her body. Feel yourself part of her and then, gradually, direct your attention to those flows in the landscape in front of you. Think about the sort of questions you want answers to. Is it more concentrated in certain places than others? Can it be detected at particular centres or along lines? Are those lines straight or sinuous or in the form of a spiral or in some other form? Is whatever you are

detecting static or fluctuating? Does it flow along any of the lines? If so, which direction is it flowing in and how fast is it flowing? If you are detecting lines, how wide are they? Are there any closely parallel lines and, if so, how many? Does all this vary over time – at different times of the day, month and year, for example? Do different dowsers detect different things?

I cannot guarantee success. It requires a certain lightness of spirit rather than grim determination. Treating it as a game seems to help. Nevertheless, it is not an easy option and your results may not be conclusive.

I want to make it clear that, as far as I am concerned, the Earth Spirit *is* a real thing which can certainly be detected by dowsing. What is not so clear, however, is what it is that we are picking up. The totality of what makes up 'the nervous system of the Earth' is so great that at any one time we can only detect a very small part of it. So, what I am saying is – by all means, dowse in the vicinity of leys which you may have found, but don't be quick to interpret the results: they may be more confusing than helpful.

Practice

Try some dowsing! A book such as *Dowsing – A Beginner's Guide* in this series will give you all the guidance that you need.

Make two rods out of an old wire coathanger, bent at right-angles to form handles and, to start with, have a go at seeing how they will react to something you know is there, such as a water-pipe. You will probably find that the rods will cross as you walk slowly over it.

If you really want to dowse earth energies, when you've had a bit of practice, go out to somewhere convenient to where you live but where you won't be disturbed or feel self-conscious. Choose somewhere such as a group of trees or an odd corner of a field – somewhere that feels right and comfortable to you.

This is your own sacred space. Get to know it, coming at different times of the day and month and at each season of the year so that you can see how the Earth, Moon and Sun cycles affect things. Dowse the whole site, especially in the vicinity of the trees, if there are any, and gradually get to know what is happening at the site on a subtle level. You may feel the need to do a survey if you want to plot your results.

This is not ley hunting as such, but it will help you tune in to leys and locate them more easily.

6 Earth Lines

A Worldwide Phenomenon

When Watkins made his initial discovery, he thought of leys as being primarily a British phenomenon. Nevertheless, he was keen to get evidence that the old straight tracks were worldwide. He soon found earlier writings and received letters from those who had read his books, giving him the confirmation he was looking for.

In Uganda, the native roads were made straight, even when ascending the steepest hills. Likewise, in the Chin district of India tracks followed the straightest line between villages. The steep climb that this frequently involved was preferred to a more level but circuitous route. In Texas, straight paths to springs were marked at intervals by two piles of stone, one bigger than the other, which could be sighted along to determine the direction to the next mark. Members of the Straight Track Club also contributed articles on tracks in such varied places as China, Assam, Palestine, Egypt, Ceylon, Tanganyika and Mexico that, in all essential respects, seemed identical to Watkins' leys – straight tracks which appeared to be aligned on prominent skyline marks.

Since Watkins' time, a lot of evidence has been presented to show that straight landscape lines, essentially similar to leys, are indeed a widespread phenomenon. But it was really only in the 1960s that the worldwide nature of linear landscape features became fully apparent.

The Lines of Nazca

The example which really caught the public imagination was the lines of Nazca, in Peru (see page vi). They could only be fully appreciated from the air and it was only with the advances in air travel that these straight lines and giant figures marked out on the Peruvian desert became widely known. This also led some to suggest fanciful notions about runways and landing grounds for space craft. But there was no denying that here were hundreds of straight lines, some over 10 kilometres (6 miles) long, going over rough terrain without deviation, together with spirals, other geometrical figures and the outlines of animals and birds. They are thought to be about a thousand years old and were formed by scraping the dark desert surface to reveal a lighter layer below. They have survived because there is virtually no rain, although tourism has taken its toll in recent years.

The purpose of the lines remains a mystery. They are certainly not all needed as trackways and there is no significant correlation with astronomical alignments. The best guess seems to be some form of ritual use.

In the New World

They were by far from being the only American lines to be discovered. A system of straight tracks was found on the Altiplano of Bolivia, high in the Andes. Some are over 32 kilometres (20 miles) long and have mounds, chapels and shrines constructed alongside them. The people walk in ritual procession along them at times of festival, worshipping the spirits of the place and leaving offerings at the shrines. In Peru there were the mysterious *ceques* – alignments of shrines radiating out from the centre of the ancient Inca capital of Cuzco (see page 60). That they had also been tracks in the past was revealed only recently by infra-red photography.

In the area around Chaco Canyon, where the four states of Arizona, New Mexico, Utah and Colorado meet, are some of the most mysterious landscape lines (see page 61). Local tradition says that

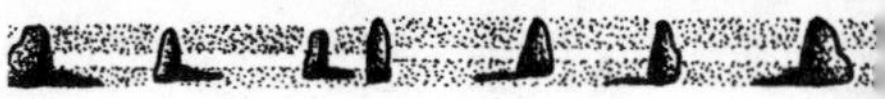

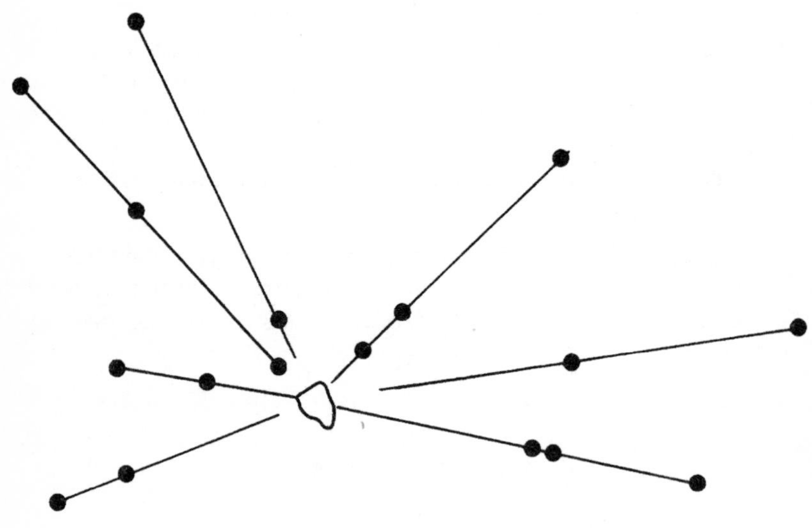

Huacas, or shrines, sited on the *ceques*, or straight paths, in Peru, leading to the Temple of the Sun in Cuzco.

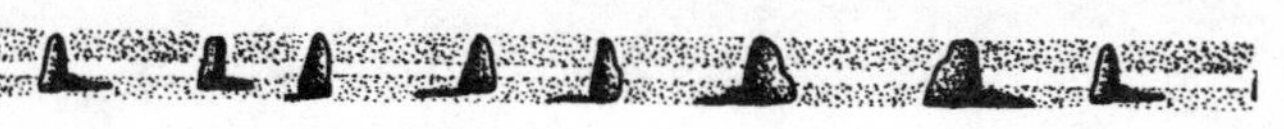

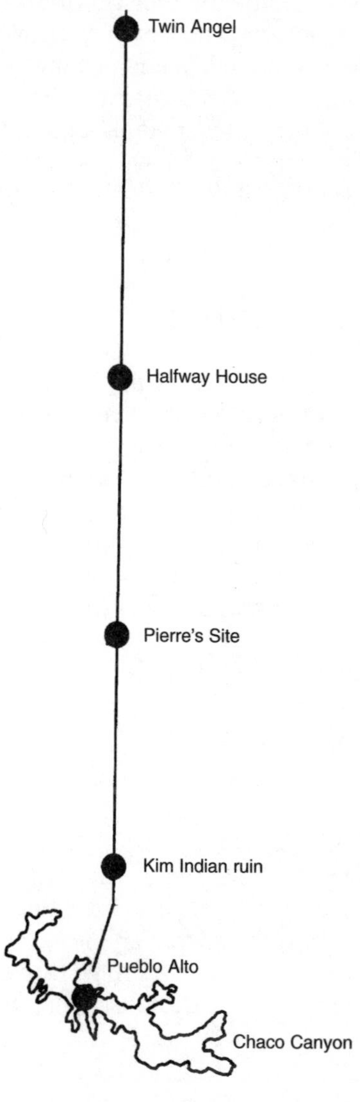

The Great North Road, one of the ancient straight tracks which focus on the Chaco Canyon in Arizona.

 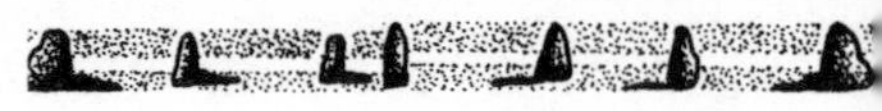

they were constructed by the Anasazi (the 'old ones'). They were broad, straight roads, now mostly only visible from the air, and were up to 48 kilometres (30 miles) long, changing direction on the ridges. Enclosures and sites containing the underground religious chambers known as *kivas* were built adjacent to the roads. The purpose of these roads is unknown, as there is no evidence of the movement of goods or, indeed, of wheeled traffic.

Ruling Lines

We tend to think that, whatever the origins of leys and lines in the landscape turn out to be, they are certainly something of a spiritual or at least benign nature. However, there is a considerable body of evidence that, in some cultures at any rate, straight lines were associated with political power and domination. The etymological clue is given by the word 'ruler', which means both something with which to draw a straight line and someone in a position of power. This has helped us to realize that straight landscape lines could be, and undoubtedly sometimes were, used as an effective tool for political domination. The system of straight tracks radiating out from the Temple of the Sun in the old Inca capital of Cuzco, where the Inca presided, is strong evidence for this.

Roman roads are another example of the ruler at the centre using straight lines to control the people. Of course, many of the Roman roads in England were constructed on alignments which already existed before the Romans came. This can be seen because the roads are laid out in straight sections with changes of direction, usually on a ridge. If the alignment of one of these straight sections is extended it will often be found to go through ancient sites such as a churchyard/sacred grove, demonstrating that the road was in origin older than Roman.

Imperial China is another example of a culture where straight lines were used to enhance central power. The emperor would sit on the Golden Throne in the Forbidden City, and from this point straight lines radiated out which could be used by the emperor but not by the

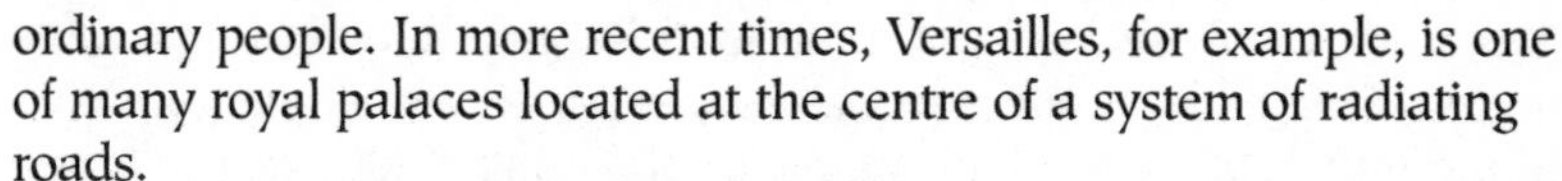

ordinary people. In more recent times, Versailles, for example, is one of many royal palaces located at the centre of a system of radiating roads.

Song Lines

Perhaps the most mysterious of all landscape lines are the song lines of the Australian aborigines. The landscape for them did not consist of areas with boundaries but of *ways through*, creating a network of lines. Mythology and tradition were enshrined in the land, often in the context of beings who came from the Earth at a waterhole (that is, a sacred site), left a trail and then went back into the Earth again. These special sites and the lines between them needed to be *sung*, which has echoes of such practices as 'beating the bounds', where particular rituals are performed at particular places to reinforce the existence of the line in the landscape and in human consciousness.

Reaves and cursuses

Even in England, there are straight landscape features which are recognized by archaeologists, such as the dead-straight prehistoric boundary lines on Dartmoor, known as *reaves* which are up to 9.5 kilometres (6 miles) long. Aerial photography has revealed an increasing number of *cursuses* – parallel prehistoric earthen banks, running straight, some for several miles. Their purpose is unknown, but they seem to be related both to rivers and to ritual sites, such as long barrows and sites currently occupied by churches.

Death roads

Old straight tracks were also found in many parts of mainland Europe and, here, the term dead-straight may be an appropriate

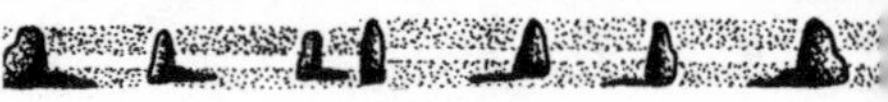

description, for these were often found to be 'death roads' – straight tracks leading to a cemetery or church. In the Netherlands, John Palmer found surviving death roads, or *doodwegen*, leading over the heathlands north of Hilversum to old burial grounds and there were also traditions of oaths being taken to ensure that the dead were carried in a straight line to be buried. These lines were also known as *lykwegen* (corpse roads) and *spokenwegen* (ghost roads).

Evidence has been found in Sweden of a straight ceremonial Viking road, known as 'Rosaring'. It was well constructed and was probably related to a funerary ritual where a chieftain's body was taken from a shrine along the road to a final resting place in a large mound.

In Britain, this link between death and straightness found expression in the corpse ways and church paths. These tracks, often but not always straight, led from outlying settlements to the parish church. It was along these that coffins were carried, and they were often marked by stones suitable as resting places for the coffin along the way. There was an old belief that by allowing a coffin to be carried over your land you had created a right of way. While this has no legal standing, it is an indication of the significance which was ascribed to these paths.

Paul Devereux gives an example of such a path in Cornwall which led to the church of St Levan's. The track is marked by a small Celtic cross and, at the boundary of the churchyard, there is another old cross and a stone the size and shape of a coffin.

A corridor of sanctity

The tradition of aligned sites involving churches seems to have continued well into mediaeval times and some of the oldest cities in England, such as London, Bristol, Cambridge, York and Norwich, have striking examples of church alignments. In York, for example, there is an alignment from the Deanery Chapter to the confluence of the Ouse and the Foss, passing through the Minster, St Sampson's, All Saints and St Mary's churches, the ancient and prominent Clifford's Tower and the site of a Templar church. Its discoverer, Brian Larkman, has called it a 'corridor of sanctity'. It is probable

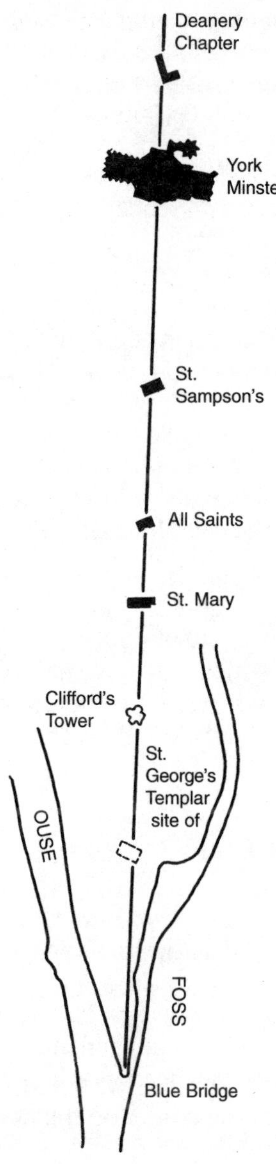

The Corridor of Sanctity, York

that the Minster and the river confluence were the 'initial points' and that the line between them can be seen as an elaboration of a church path, to the extent that new churches, when needed, were built on the already sanctified line.

Ghost roads

Straight tracks often seem to be associated with the less tangible side of life – ghosts, fairies, witches and the like – and we shall see in the next chapter why this might be so. Ulrich Magin has drawn attention to the German *Geisterwege* or ghost paths. These ran in a straight line over mountains, valleys and marshes, starting or ending at a cemetery. Ghosts (thought of as being the spirits of the dead) were believed to use these paths, as also were nature spirits. It was thought that they could be seen by those who were sensitive.

In Britain there are also examples of ghosts associated with paths leading to churchyards. Folklore researcher Jeremy Harte has found evidence in Dorset of such haunted paths, particularly including sightings of black dogs, which may have links with legends about the Wild Hunt, which can be seen as a particularly vivid manifestation which could give rise to folk tales about ghost paths.

Faery paths

The Irish 'faery paths' are another example of such a tradition. The faeries were believed to follow straight paths between their faery castles, or *raths*, and it was considered unlucky to obstruct or build anything over one of these lines. There is a well-known case where the owner of a new house was having bad luck. On consulting a wise woman, she advised him that the house had been constructed over a faery path. He cut the corner off the house and his bad luck ceased.

All of these examples, plus a wealth of other evidence built up by researchers and writers such as Paul Devereux and in the pages of *The Ley Hunter* makes it abundantly clear not only that straight tracks and other landscape lines are a worldwide phenomenon, but that they are associated both with temporal power and with the Otherworld – the world of spirit. We shall explore that link in the next chapter.

PRACTICE

Visit your local library and read up about the folklore, legends and traditions of your area and ask the older inhabitants as well! They are often a source of valuable information that may never have reached any of the books.

The information that you have gathered will be useful if you want to go further into what is called Earth Mysteries, but for the present, see if there are any traditions of straight paths, perhaps going to and from a church, or folk memory of alignment, or anything else that strikes your eye.

Journals such as *The Ley Hunter* may be interested if you write up what you find.

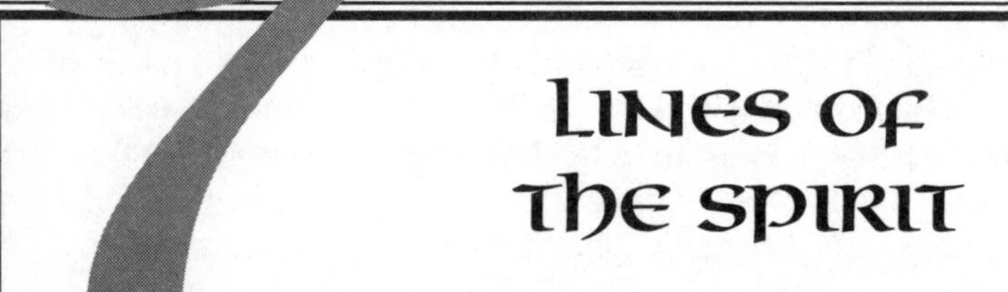

7 Lines of the Spirit

Consciousness and Straightness

From the start, one of the commonest arguments against Watkins' ideas about leys went something like this:

'People didn't walk in straight lines. They weren't idiots – they took the easiest path across the country, the line of least resistance, going round *hills and other obstacles rather than over them. Anyway, we know all about prehistoric trackways – they followed the chalk ridges and were anything but straight.'*

Now, all this sounded eminently reasonable to mid twentieth-century English archaeologists and it was only when incontrovertible evidence came forward in the 1970s from writers such as Tony Morrison of the existence of long straight tracks in the Bolivian Altiplano which were, in Paul Devereux's phrase, 'terrain oblivious', that a new generation of archaeologists, with more open minds, began to concede the point. If they exist in present-day Bolivia there is, in essence, no reason why they should not have existed in prehistoric Britain. They didn't actually go so far as to call them leys, but they did begin to look more seriously at other straight landscape features such as cursuses, reaves and astronomical alignments.

The difference really is all to do with *consciousness*. We cannot transplant our late twentieth-century world view onto the prehistoric peoples and expect them to think, and feel, the same way as us. In

many important ways their consciousness was different and what we have to do, and it is probably one of the most difficult things, is to try to think in the way that the ancient people may have done. What seems peculiar to us may have seemed perfectly natural to them. But we do have some clues.

First of all, it's very difficult to change our consciousness if we stay as outside observers. We have to get *involved*, going to the sites and along the leys, and consciously move into a different way of seeing things. To help us understand what is involved, we can gain a lot from surviving peoples who retain something of this level of consciousness, such as the Australian aborigines, the native Americans and the shamans of northern Europe and Siberia. One of the problems until fairly recently was that the only material available was written by anthropologists who had a largely Christian background. They did not really understand the concepts that they were being told and had no words which were adequate to describe them. The result in most cases was a rather unsatisfactory text which failed to explain the essential experiences.

However, things have improved recently and we have begun to be aware, at least partially, of what the ancient peoples' world-view, mind-set, or level of consciousness may have been.

First of all, they were far more sensitive than we are and had a highly developed psychic ability which made them far more aware of their place in nature – a part of it rather than separate from it. This awareness of their integrity with the rest of the Earth, their attunement with the land, meant that they could move across the surface of the Earth harmoniously. Indeed, they could be said to have a ritual and pilgrimage-oriented view of doing things, not just a practical one.

An example of such a world-view is provided by the Kogi Indians of northern Colombia, who live on the relatively inaccessible mountain mass of the Sierra Nevada de Santa Marta. From a young age, they carry out certain techniques which enable them to see the spirit world: a place they call *aluna*. Their villages are linked with straight paths, but they are also aware of paths which only exist in *aluna* – what we might call 'spirit paths'.

Spirit paths

Such paths can only be perceived in an altered state of consciousness, so let us look at straight landscape lines with the perspective of consciousness. Both Watkins' leys and the South American lines have chapels and wayside crosses. The church paths and death roads are to do with the passage of the individual to the next world, and ghost and faery paths emphasize the link with the Otherworld.

All these associations can be summed up in a unifying concept – that of the sanctity of the straight landscape line and its essential function as allowing the passage of the spirit. This is the conclusion of Paul Devereux, former Editor of *The Ley Hunter*, who achieved a breakthrough in understanding the purpose of archaic landscape lines, something which allowed sense to be made of otherwise disparate material.

For most of us, the out-of-body experience – astral travel – is something unusual, although I suspect that many of our dreams are actually such experiences. We call them by one name, but actually our dreams are several different things – processing of the day's experiences, symbolic communications from our subconscious and memories originating in a previous lifetime being some of them. Another is undoubtedly astral travel, or out-of-body experience.

Shamanic journeying

But for the ancient peoples and those who live close to the earth, such experiences are literally just part of life. Certain special individuals, known as *shamans* in Siberia but known in all ancient cultures, had particular skill at leaving the body and journeying in this way, frequently transforming into a bird or animal. In the shamanic trance of the San people of southern Africa, the individual 'transforms' into an antelope, and then leaves his or her body and flies. It is this flight of the soul that seems to relate to the landscape lines.

Devereux found evidence that shamanic journeying, where the soul or spirit appears to leave the physical body and go on a journey, occurs along particular lines in the landscape and that such lines are straight. It is a point of debate as to whether such journeying is actual or symbolic. I believe it to be a real phenomenon, for verifiable information can be obtained during such an experience. Either way, particular landscape lines and the places on them are seen as being sanctified by such journeying and are subsequently marked by such features as shrines and by paths being worn along the lines themselves by those who see virtue in following them.

While I have not experienced anything as dramatic as that, I have certainly visited landscapes in my dreams which I later recognized when visiting them physically. Those dreams seemed to have a special quality, as if I was moving above the ground and propelling myself by pushing my chest forward – difficult to describe but very real. This leads me to the conclusion that when straight flight across landscape is being described in legend, folklore and mythology, it is actual *astral travel* that is taking place.

This inevitably leads us on to ask the question 'Why does shamanic flight occur along certain lines?' There are actually many different possibilities and little work has been done beyond the recognition of the paths. Perhaps they are lines of desire, where the shaman visits in spirit an already sacred site or journeys from one to another. Or perhaps these are truly the veins, arteries and nervous system of the Earth that can readily be detected by those who are in a state of heightened awareness.

Witch flight paths

Take the example of the witch. In the popular imagination, witches are supposed to ride through the air on broomsticks. In fact, this is probably a reference to 'flying ointments' which mediaeval witches rubbed on to their bodies. They contained hallucinogenic alkaloids

which gave the feeling of flight and, indeed, may have aided actual out-of-body experiences. The flight was often experienced in the guise of some animal such as a goose, and this probably links to phrases like 'as the crow flies', which brings together the concepts of straightness and bird flight.

Witches were traditionally supposed to have followed certain paths straight across the countryside on the way to their Sabbats. The folklorist Ethel Rudkin tells of a witch who was flying from a temple above Anwick, in Lincolnshire, with some stolen stones. She was shot at by some shepherds and dropped the coffin–shaped stones, which could still be seen at Ewerby Waithe Common. On plotting this line on a map, an alignment can be noted between Dorrington Church, the Drake Stone (a large natural boulder) at Anwick and Ewerby Waithe Common.

Now, such a shamanic flight, if real, or even if undertaken in the rich imaginative realms of the unconscious mind, could be translated into the physical landscape and marked, either at the instructions of the shaman or by those who may have witnessed the flight through psychic vision, either on one occasion or on a regular basis.

These straight spirit lines are a strong part of local tradition in much of the world. Often they are not marked physically in the landscape and remain what we might call a cultural concept. We have already seen the examples of the Irish faery paths, the Chinese *lung mei* and the aluna paths of the Kogi. While not marked physically, people knew where they were and respected them. Looked at in this way, such varied elements of folklore as black dog paths, the roads taken by the Wild Hunt, and even Santa Claus and his reindeer, can be seen primarily as spirit paths.

PRACTICE

The implication in this chapter is that, to understand the concept of spirit paths fully, it is necessary to change one's consciousness.

We can probably never do it fully because of our cultural conditioning, but we can make the attempt, and this is what I want you to do.

Go out somewhere, preferably at night, where you are unlikely to be disturbed, ideally where street lights and traffic sounds are not too obtrusive. Take a friend with you if you would otherwise feel too vulnerable or afraid.

Find a comfortable spot to sit down, preferably with your back to a tree and relax, allowing your breathing to slow naturally.

What I want you to try and do is to feel what it would be like to be someone who was living at the time when the leys were laid out; one who was sensitive to all the animals and plants; one who could be aware of the subtle dimensions of life and the unity of all existence.

I want you to really 'get under the skin' of such a person, so you can feel what they were feeling and see things through their eyes.

You may find that certain thoughts or images come to mind: allow them to flow through until you feel ready to come back to the modern world.

This is the sort of exercise you can carry out as often as you want to. What you learn from it might be difficult to put into words, but you will gain an intuitive understanding of what was going on and this should help you to realize something of what 'the sanctity of the straight' is about, for here we are dealing with very deep images and experiences which are beyond words.

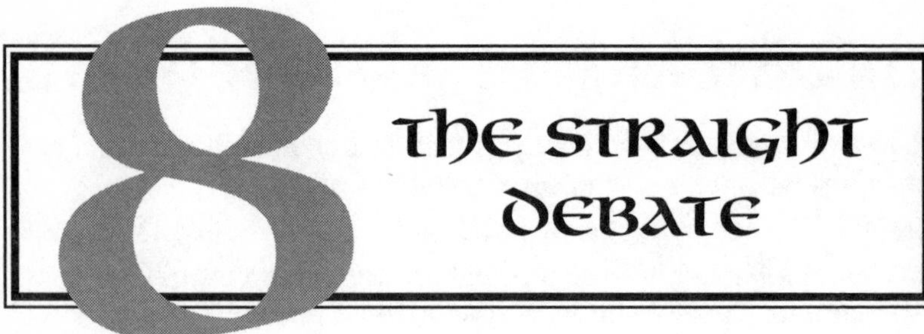

8 The Straight Debate

'They didn't walk in straight lines!'

We've looked at ideas about them from Watkins' initial discovery onwards, but before we open the debate about whether they were traders' tracks, lines of earth energy, spirit paths or whatever, there is a much more fundamental question which needs to be asked: do leys actually exist?

This is not just a philosophical question. You've found an alignment of sites on the map and traced the line in the field, probably getting very muddy in the process! Now you want to know – is it real?

Of course, as with all new ideas, Watkins' claims for the existence of leys were not enthusiastically taken up by the archaeologists of the time. It is perhaps inevitable that controversy surrounded leys right from the start. Certainly his contemporaries in the archaeological field were highly critical.

'Prehistoric people didn't walk in straight lines – they took the easiest path. They were just as lazy as we are!'

In answer to this, we can certainly now put forward the arguments set out in the previous chapter that straight tracks essentially similar to leys can be found throughout the world and that, to understand motives for their construction, we need to change our consciousness to approach more nearly that of the people who made them: their values may well have been very different from our own.

'They weren't all there at the same time!'

One of the other arguments which has always been used against the ley theory is that the variety of different markers which Watkins counted as indicators of the presence of a ley can be very different in terms of age, from prehistoric burial mounds to mediaeval churches.

'You're using mixed markers – they weren't all there at the same time, so the lines are meaningless!'

To answer this, let us take a parallel example. In most of our historic towns we may find old buildings, but what is far more certain is that we will find old street lines. The buildings are likely to come and go over the years, getting demolished and rebuilt with the vagaries of fashion, but the plots on which they were built remain largely the same and the street lines frequently survive into modern times.

So it is, Watkins claimed (and it has since been verified on many occasions), with ley mark-points. Churches – one of the main focuses for criticism – are known to have been built on pagan sites, as we saw in Chapter 1.

'It doesn't mean a thing!'

Of course it was argued that leys were only coincidental. The English countryside was so full of features that any arbitrary line was bound to go through a few of them, just by chance.

'You're bound to get alignments of sites in a crowded country like England – there's so many of them. It doesn't mean a thing.'

One of the arguments against leys was that you could line up other totally unrelated things, including Woolworths' stores and telephone boxes. Now, most of those who claimed this never actually bothered to do it, but it is an interesting exercise because it does show the extent to which alignment occurs naturally among

totally unrelated things and warns us that just because sites line up doesn't necessarily mean that the alignment is of significance, far less that they are on a ley.

On the face of it, this is an argument that should be possible to be settled using statistical analysis, particularly in the age of computers. Put at its simplest, we ask what would be the number of alignments between a scatter of random points on a map and how does this compare to the number of alignments of real sites actually found.

In response to criticism, Watkins did this himself. He took the Ordnance Survey 1 inch to 1 mile (1.5 centimetres to 1 kilometre) map which covered the Andover area of Hampshire. He noted that there were 51 churches on the map. He circled them and systematically tested them for alignments. He found eight four-point lines and one five-point. What he then did was to compare this with a chance distribution. He took a sheet of paper the same size and shape as the map and put 51 crosses at random. On examining the alignments in this case, he found that the number of three-point lines was more or less the same in each case, but there was only one four-point and no five-point lines. He concluded from this that a line with four or more churches on it was highly likely to be deliberate rather than accidental.

But as you multiply the type of mark-points you are considering, such as mounds, crossroads and so on, so the number of points necessary to make a convincing ley increases. For practical purposes, and including the various mark-points which are likely to be shown on Ordnance Survey 1:50,000 scale maps, five points accurately aligned is the minimum you should work to.

In more recent years, computers have been brought in to help with this work. In the 1970s, Pat Gadsby and Chris Hutton-Squire looked at the alignments of standing stones in the West Penwith area of Cornwall which John Michell had written about in his book *The Old Stones of Lands End*. The grid references of 53 standing stones and other sites were fed into the computer, which found the alignments between them. Random number tables were then used to generate an imaginary set of 53 sites but with the same general distribution over the survey area, and the computer being used again to find

alignments between these. The analysis showed that the chances against getting the number of alignments which actually existed were at least 160 to 1 and this result spurred on further research.

Taking the Saintbury ley that we have already looked at, for example, statistician Robert Forrest analysed it and found it to be 'significant at the 1 per cent level' – in other words, it was probably deliberate.

One important lesson that we can learn from statistical analysis is that a certain number of alignments will occur by chance, in the normal course of events. In other words, the sites on them were never deliberately aligned. We must expect to find some of these in our ley hunting, so we have to find some way of 'filtering out' these 'chance' alignments so that we can concentrate on the 'genuine' leys. There is no easy or foolproof way to do this but, as with many things, it becomes easier with experience.

A good indication is the length of the ley. A relatively short one, like the Saintbury ley, is more likely to be deliberate than an alignment with the same number of points stretching the whole length of the map. Another indication is to look at what Watkins called 'confirmation points' – are there any stretches of road along the line? Do they change direction as they cross the line? Does the line go through crossroads and road junctions with regularity?

But the only *real* test of the validity of a ley is *fieldwork*. If you find all sorts of interesting things exactly on the line, such as field gates, solitary Scots pines, unexplained earthworks, ponds and so on, then your confidence in what you have found will inevitably build up.

The more we look at the statistical analysis of leys, however, the more problems seem to emerge. In practice, there are so many factors that affect the significance of a ley that it would be difficult to take them all into account. If you have ever looked for leys on a map you will know the feeling of *rightness* which comes when you find one. It's like when you meet a friend in the street. You know it's them, but if asked to describe them you would probably find it difficult to go into sufficient detail for anyone else to draw a picture purely from your description. Similarly, the fact that we know when we've found a ley is based on far more than just the number of

points and the accuracy of alignment. It's something ultimately indefinable to do with the grain of the land. What you are doing in making this sort of judgement is actually taking into account a lot of subtle factors which are difficult or impossible to identify but which make sense in terms of our understanding of the landscape.

And that is just the point. To prove the existence of leys statistically will probably always remain just out of reach.

'So, what are Leys?'

What it all means is another matter, which has been tackled since the time of the Straight Track Club, the members of which did not all accept Watkins' theories as established truth.

We might start by posing a simple question: what is a ley? But, like many of the simplest questions, it has no easy answer. We could give Watkins' definition and say something like 'an alignment of ancient sites marking the position of an old straight traders' track'. But even thinking for a short time about what I have so far put forward, we realize that there are so many unanswered questions that prevent us from giving such a straightforward response. Controversy on the origin, meaning and purpose of leys has been rife ever since Watkins' first book on the subject in 1922. In fact, in my view, most of this argument is quite unnecessary, as I hope to show.

So, what *are* leys? Are they, as Watkins thought, the remnants of a network of tracks designed to make trade easier in hostile country?

Or could they be the survivors of some ancient system for making sense of the land by 'taking its measure' – an early survey? Or the results of an attempt at play – the joy of making patterns, at landscape scale?

Perhaps human attempts to fix the positions of a subtle dynamic system – the energy body of the Earth?

Or maybe they are not, after all, so benign and represent traces of a system of central political, military and religious control.

They could even represent the paths taken by fairies and other inhabitants of the Otherworld or the memory of the spirit flights of shamans, witches or those passing over to the next world.

One could say that leys are all these things – and more. Before we go any further we must look at some other ideas about leys which can be seen as being developments of the 'earth energy' concept.

Meshes and Grids?

Whilst we can think of the Earth as a goddess, having certain characteristics in common with ourselves, such as life, movement and the flow of energy around our bodies, there are also differences so we should not expect to see exact parallels in every respect.

Some people have extrapolated from localized dowsing findings while others have worked from maps and have come up with a whole series of 'energy grids' ultimately covering the whole planet. Those published (and there is a great variety of them, none of which seem to relate to each other) are very regular, either based on a polyhedron superimposed on the Earth or more localized parallel or star systems.

Now, the Earth is not really like this. It *is* alive and it is rich in its subtlety, and to impose these impoverished rigid structures on a living being says more about our need for artificial and simplified order than about the subtle anatomy of the Earth. I was guilty of this myself in my early days, but I hope I have developed a little in wisdom and maturity since then!

Long-distance Leys?

As an example of this way of thinking, we can look at one of the ideas to emerge from the 1960s revival of interest – the concept of long-distance leys, which was really a development of Tyler's ideas into what became known as 'landscape geometry'. One of the best

known 'long-distance leys' is the 'St. Michael Line', originally postulated by John Michell, which runs from St Michael's Mount in Cornwall to the Norfolk coast, through such geomantic centres as Brent Tor, Glastonbury, Avebury stone circle and Bury St Edmunds. The many churches and other sites claimed to be on the line are not precisely aligned, and it has been described as a 'geomantic corridor', a concept which implies significance in landscape terms without statistical precision.

There was much enthusiasm for 'long-distance leys' in the 1960s, and I was responsible for some of it myself, drawing grids of parallel lines across the whole country – a lot of fun to do, but I am quite certain now that there was absolutely no correlation with any real pattern in the landscape: it was totally my own *imagination*.

Subconscious siting?

Another way in which alignment of sites could occur is by what Jimmy Goddard has called 'subconscious siting'. If we postulate the existence of a straight spirit line, energy line, or whatever, then ancient peoples could well have been sensitive to this, either consciously or unconsciously. They may have sited sacred structures or planted tree clumps because they felt the spots chosen were in some way 'special' without knowing quite why, or it may have been a totally unconscious process.

There are enough examples of modern churches, memorials and such like falling on otherwise well-documented leys, to make it likely that some such process is in operation. Nigel Pennick has drawn attention to the American Military Cemetery at Madingley, near Cambridge, which has been laid out (quite unconsciously) with its main axis along a ley which Alfred Watkins had previously found and published in his book *Archaic Tracks Round Cambridge*.

Another example of subconscious siting can be found on a ley which I plotted in East Yorkshire from the church at Sproatley eastwards towards the sea at Grimston. It has a former isolated country public house and a remote Methodist chapel exactly on the line.

The cultural context

It is also interesting that many of the early theories reflected the lives of those writing about them.

Take Alfred Watkins. He worked for the family firm, which was engaged in brewing and flour milling and he was the one who came up with the idea of traders' tracks.

Major Tyler was a military man in a position of authority and his theories about the geometrical arrangement of ancient sites suggests a high degree of central control and discipline to achieve the observed patterns.

Kenneth Koop was a surveyor by training and it was he who promoted the theory that leys may have been part of an early survey.

Tony Wedd, the wartime pilot, was the one who saw the landscape lines as flight paths for space craft, navigating by the pine clump landmarks.

Now, I am not suggesting that these ideas are invalidated because of the background of their protagonists: that it is simply a case of these observers believing what they wanted to believe. But it *is* true that the cultural context in which we live has a definite influence over our approach to the subject and to our ideas about them. This is still the case today, whether we recognize it or not: we are a product of the twentieth century and it is hardly surprising if our ideas and experience of linearity in the landscape reflect this.

One aspect of a changing consciousness is a growth in our ability to recognize that the various theories about leys are not necessarily incompatible. In fact, I hold firmly to the view that there is no incompatibility between the various theories and there is consequently no need to choose between them.

As an example, one of the strongest controversies about leys in recent years has been between the supporters of the 'spirit line' theory and those who consider that leys mark lines of earth energy. Now, my immediate, though perhaps rather flippant, response to this is to ask the protagonists whether they have experienced spirit

and energy and whether they can tell the difference between them, because I certainly can't!

To put it perhaps rather more clearly, 'spirit' seems to be used in a historical context, in dealing with folklore and ritual practices and beliefs, whereas 'energy' (where it is other than pure theory and imposing patterns on maps) is usually referred to in the context of present-day experience – what people have felt at and in the vicinity of sacred sites, ley mark-points and on leys themselves.

The cultural context is very different, but that does not mean that the underlying experience is different. Essentially we are dealing with the human response to the landscape at a level beyond the physical, particularly the type of response which finds expression in linearity.

It has been argued that talk of 'earth energies' is a product of our present-day technological civilization and has no place in what we might call the prehistoric mind-set. But every culture approaches reality from its own direction using terms and concepts with which it is familiar. So Arthur Lawton wrote about a mesh consisting of 'tubes of force'; Dion Fortune referred to 'lines of force'; to Tony Wedd they were 'magnetic currents'; and today 'earth energy' or 'spirit lines' are the usually favoured terms. All these words effectively disguise the fact that we really know very little about what we are experiencing – except that we *are* experiencing it.

My own experiences at the Hart Stone, in Lastingham Crypt and at numerous other places, and those of others who have written about their own experiences, reveal something which is real; which can affect us physically, mentally, emotionally and spiritually; which feels alive (because it flows and fluctuates) and which can, at least *some* of the time and in *some* places, be experienced as flowing in straight channels. Now, while the *expression* may be that of modern culture, the *experience* is universal and would be familiar, I maintain, to anyone from an earlier culture who may have expressed it in terms of spirit lines.

But perhaps we should be less concerned about asking the question 'What are leys?' What if it was the wrong question? Certainly to talk about 'leys' rather suggests one system of alignments throughout the world with identity of origin, design and use. It almost certainly never was that way and the questions we should really be posing are 'Where can we find examples of linearity in the landscape?' and 'What significance do they have?'

It seems clear that leys are not just one thing, brought into being by some centralized organization. Indeed, it might be better to replace the concept of the ley with the idea of 'linearity in the landscape', or some such phrase. It is obvious from what we have seen that linear landscape features, whether they manifest as roads, alignments of sites, ways for the passage of spirits, ghosts or faeries (or detectable lines of what, for want of a better word, has been called 'earth energy') crop up all over the world in widely differing cultures and eras.

I hope that I have given enough examples to show that purposeful linearity is indeed a worldwide phenomenon, but not necessarily one having a single origin.

practice

Think about the leys that you have discovered and the time you spent exploring them in the field.

What do you *feel* that they are? Open yourself to all the different ideas about leys which you have read about so far (and any that you have come up with yourself).

Stretch your mind to see how far you can reconcile ideas that you might have thought of as being incompatible.

And think about the two ways in which ideas come into being: someone tells you things (the first way – the so-called diffusionist theory) and you think them up for yourself (the second way – what has been called 'spontaneous generation').

Some of the most fundamental things, like love and sheltering from danger, don't have to be taught: others, like French and Christianity, have to be learned.

Think about which category leys fall into and what the implications are of seeing them in this way.

9 Straightness and Life

The Ley as an Archetype

So, leys are not just one thing. Indeed, 'leys', as classically defined by Watkins, may not exist at all, or at least be a very specific phenomenon in a restricted area. Straight tracks and alignments are part of the cultural history and geography of many parts of the world but they are not, in any sense, part of one system.

The straight landscape line is certainly a theme in literature. Bunyan's *The Pilgrim's Progress* can be read at one level as being a journey along a ley, passing various landmarks and waymarks *en route*. An example which shows a deeply held and largely unconscious belief in the significance of the straight line is provided by Hilaire Belloc's *The Path to Rome*. On his conversion to Catholicism, the author set out to walk to Rome from his home in France, keeping as near as possible to a straight line.

Let us see what we can make of it all and try to discern some common ground from the mass of material available to us. Why was there this obsession with straightness in the landscape? The worldwide nature of linear landscape features and concepts rather suggests that we are looking at something having a universal quality deep within each individual, something which springs up spontaneously within people when they relate to the landscape: the need to superimpose, or to become aware of, straightness and the creation of landscape lines.

This is what is called an *archetype*, a fundamental principle of human experience, and something which is the common inheritance of us all, originating in what Jung called 'the collective unconscious'. If this is so, then straightness in the landscape needn't have just one explanation: it can be multi-determined, coming up whenever people need to express things in landscape terms, whether it be trackways, surveys, or whatever. This variety is its richness and strength, which is what one would expect of an archetype.

Of course it is very important not to overemphasize straightness, for we live in a 'wiggly world'. Certainly straightness is not the only archetype which can be translated into landscape terms, and we might think, for example, of the circle, as represented by the 'fairy ring', the mating track of the roe deer or the simple crop circle. Others include the spiral and the curve; the principle of 'seeing without being seen' which lies at the heart of Prospect/Refuge theory and the cardinal points, from which are derived the grid and the square and many of the elaborations of sacred geometry.

We can all think of examples of straightness in nature, such as the reflection of the sun setting over a calm sea, or its rays shining from behind a cloud, shadow paths from a setting sun down a falling hillside, the stalk of wheat, the high waterfall, the surface of scree from a mountain and the horizon viewed over a flat landscape.

But these are the exceptions: nature is essentially curved, sinuous, even wiggly! That is the nature of life as we know it and it is that which Wilhelm Reich elaborated on in his researches into orgone energy and which he called 'cosmic superimposition'.

It seems to follow that linearity in the landscape is predominantly human – that people have had some urge to make straight lines across the land over a long period of time and throughout the world. We have seen that all ancient philosophies and religions have as their basis the principle that there is a unity underlying all existence. If one can reach the state of realization of this 'cosmic consciousness' as Bucke described it, the Universe is experienced as a unity in which time and space cease to have any meaning. It follows that, at the deepest level of experience, there is no distance between any two points, or indeed, any two people: they are absolutely together. We have all heard the saying that 'the shortest distance between two points is a straight line'. This is true in the

physical world, but in the deeper world that the shaman inhabits that distance can be eliminated and there can be perfect psychic communication between two people at a distance, perfect clairvoyance of a distant place, or whatever.

So could the straight line in the landscape be a physical symbol of this deeper experience of communication? The straight line may have become the recognized physical symbol of that link between any two points because it was the closest approximation to, and, therefore, a good symbol to represent, that deep spiritual link which transcends time and space. Back in the everyday world of time and space, this cosmic consciousness had to be symbolized by many things, including birds of various descriptions. The transcendence of space, which was an important component of that consciousness, could be symbolized by that which most nearly brings the two points together – the straight line.

As we have seen, there are points in the landscape, the traditional sacred sites, where touching the Otherworld can more easily occur – holy wells, stones, hilltops, for example – the power of which is attested in worldwide myth, legend and folklore, as well as in present-day investigations and experiences. From this concept of the straight line between two sacred points as a symbol of the Otherworld, we get such beliefs as legends of secret tunnels and the sacredness of the old straight trackways and crossroads.

The Moon and the Apple Tree

A different way of looking at straightness in the landscape occurred to me recently. I won't call it a revelation, but it had some of the same qualities. This idea came vividly when I was out in the garden sitting on an old swing and looking into the sky. I could see the newly sprouting buds on the nearby apple tree silhouetted against the Moon. My thoughts turned to the alignment between my eye, the apple bud and the Moon, and I suddenly realized that while these points were undoubtedly in alignment I was not perceiving them as a straight line: I saw them as being together – what astrologers would call a conjunction. When we think of alignment in the landscape our mind immediately goes to the straight line – drawing a possible ley on a map, lining up churches or whatever. So much so that it is often difficult to perceive things as they actually are. While we can represent a ley by a straight line on a map, the points on it, when viewed perhaps from a high point on the line, will appear together.

Look again at the drawing of the view along a ley on page 24. Don't look at it as a drawing, but as a collection of abstract shapes. We know that they are all a different distance from us. The stone circle is in the foreground; the church spire is in the middle distance; and the hilltop clump is in the far distance. Our intellect, backed up by the map, sees them as being in alignment, but our eyes, seeing them as abstract shapes, see them grouped together in one direction.

So looked at from another viewpoint (literally), the straight landscape line is not only a symbol for a universal archetype, *it is an actual physical demonstration of that principle.*

My revelation on looking at the Moon and the apple tree also made me realize vividly the possible significance of alignments to horizon points marking the rising of Sun, Moon and other bodies. The coincidence (conjunction) of sites in the landscape with a celestial body could be seen as being a powerful symbol for the integration of planetary energies with the landscape, as astrologers would recognize. These lines would naturally link places where the Earth Spirit, however defined, was strong and where the 'veil between the worlds' was correspondingly thinnest. They would also link human settlements to such places. That they might also mark straight flows of energy across the Earth's surface, between such centres, would seem to be undeniable, although straightness is only one of the characteristics of the living Earth, which, being living, is subject to constant change.

Conclusion

But, enough of philosophizing! Ley hunting is essentially a practical activity – getting out whenever possible into the countryside, seeing what is actually there with new eyes. Now that you have read this book the landscape will never seem quite the same ever again and it may even lead you in some quite unexpected directions. So, be prepared!

Practice

Go out for a walk and see things as they actually are! This is the advice given to aspiring artists: draw what you see and not what you think you see!

So, go and pay another visit to some of the ley mark-points that you have found and look along the ley with new eyes. See the conjunction – the coming together of landscape features – and notice how the third dimension – elevation – often brings points together in a remarkable way.

Watch the sun or moon rise and, better still, turn round and see your own shadow path indicate a living line on the Earth's surface.

Appendix: Waymarks to Further Study

I hope that this book has encouraged you to go out ley hunting in the countryside. You will learn far more from walking along an ancient path towards a clump of Scots pines on the skyline, suddenly discovering a markstone under a hedge or an earthwork exactly on the line than you will from reading books.

But, for good measure, I shall give you some titles anyway!

The classic texts, of course, are those by Alfred Watkins. His main work, originally published in 1925, is *The Old Straight Track* (reprinted Garnstone Press, 1970 and Abacus, 1974). Profusely illustrated with his marvellous photographs, this tells the story of Watkins' discovery, concentrating on the leys that he found in his native Herefordshire and Welsh borders.

Watkins' next book, *The Ley Hunter's Manual* (reprinted Turnstone, 1983) appeared two years later. It is really an outline of the ley theory with an emphasis on practical ley hunting.

A more recent overview of the whole subject is *Lines on the Landscape* by Nigel Pennick and Paul Devereux (Hale, 1989). This goes into considerable detail about linear landscape features in different parts of the world and shows the development of ideas about them.

Paul Devereux is also the author of *Shamanism and the Mystery Lines* (Quantum, 1992), the main exposition of the 'spirit lines' theories about leys.

The New Ley Hunter's Guide, again by Paul Devereux (Gothic Image 1994), gives a lot of detail on how to go about ley hunting, describes some example leys and gives an authoritative account of the latest theories.

For looking at leys in the wider context, my own *The Elements of Earth Mysteries* (Element, 1991, reissued 1998) and Teresa Moorey's *Earth Mysteries – A Beginner's Guide* (Hodder & Stoughton, 1998) are good introductions.

Although published almost a quarter of a century ago, John Michell's *The Earth Spirit* (Thames and Hudson 1975) is an evocative and finely illustrated description of what have been called 'earth energies' – the manifestations of the living Earth.

To keep up-to-date with the latest ideas, new books and events, the best thing to do is to subscribe to *The Ley Hunter*, the premier magazine in the field, which has been published since 1965. Details can be obtained from *The Ley Hunter*, PO Box 180, Stroud, GL5 1YH, United Kingdom. *The Ley Hunter* also has a web site at **http://www.leyhunter.com**

There are several local earth mysteries and ley research groups which organize regular meetings and conferences (often called 'moots') together with ley walking days and weekends. These are good ways to meet others interested in the subject. Details can be obtained from *The Ley Hunter*, but one covering the north of England and Scotland which has been active since 1979 is the *Northern Earth Mysteries Group*, c/o John Billingsley, 10 Jubilee Street, Mytholmroyd, Hebden Bridge, HX7 5NP, United Kingdom.

I have given only a small selection of books about leys and journals devoted to the subject. There are many more, but I didn't want to overwhelm you! Most of the books mentioned have very good bibliographies.

If you read at least some of those I have given, plus *The Ley Hunter*, you will then be in a better position to go further into the subject and follow your particular interests.